The Nordic Spirit: Peacemakers

Edited by Christine Ingebritsen and Howard Rockstad

The authors wish to express their thanks
for the enduring efforts of
Howard Rockstad
to coordinate our works into
the first ever publication of the Nordic Spirit Symposium
held at California Lutheran University
by the Scandinavian American Cultural and Historical Foundation.

Copyright 2014 by the Scandinavian American Cultural and Historical Foundation

Sentia Publishing Company has the exclusive rights to reproduce this work, to prepare derivative works from this work, to publicly distribute this work, to publicly perform this work, and to publicly display this work.

All rights reserved. No part of this publication may be reproduced, stored in a retrieval system, or transmitted, in any form or by any means, electronic, mechanical, photocopying, recording, or otherwise, without the prior written permission of the copyright owner.

Printed in the United States of America.

ISBN 978-0-9903026-5-0

Dedication

This volume is dedicated to the memory of Carl Allan Carlson (1931-2012), who suggested this Nordic Spirit symposium topic of peacemakers and humanitarians, often spoke of the importance of inclusion of the two Scandinavian Americans Earl Warren and Warren Christopher, and frequently stated his feelings that peacemakers and humanitarians was the most important topic for the Nordic Spirit symposium series.

Table of Contents

Introduction   *vii*

Preface   *ix*

The Power of Scandinavia   ***1***

    Soft Power In Four Distinct Issue-Areas   7

    The Retention of Universalism   8

    Conflict Resolution and the Promotion of Peace   9

    Harnessing Technology for Social Purposes   9

    Scandinavia and the Global Environment   10

    How Does Scandinavian Studies Connect Young Scholars to the Study of Power?   11

    What Other Projects Reflect the Priorities of Our Teaching and Learning?   12

    What's Hot in Cold State Studies?   12

    In Conclusion   13

Fridtjof Nansen:
From Polar Explorer to Humanitarian Hero   ***15***

    The Rise of a Hero   15

    Humanitarian Engagement: Prisoners of War   18

    Famine Relief   19

    Refugees   20

    Achievements   22

    Literature: 25

Peace through Justice and Reconciliation:
The Legacy of Nathan Söderblom   ***27***

    I. The Career of Nathan Söderblom   28

    II. Nathan Söderblom on Church Unity and World Peace   32

    III. Söderblom's Views on Social Issues   34

    IV. Conference on Life and Work, Stockholm, 1925   36

    V. The Place of Söderblom in History   38

From Neutrality to Peacemaking.
The Dangerous Challenges of Mediation:
Folke Bernadotte and Dag Hammarskjöld   ***41***

    Folke Bernadotte   46

    Bernadotte's Last Mission   47

    Dag Hammarskjöld 1905-1961   49

    From Passive Neutrality to Active non-alignment   51

Nordic Influences and Nordic Sons   ***53***

    Warren Christopher (1925-2011): The Indispensable Man   54

    Earl Warren (1891-1974): Equal Justice Under Law   56

Appendix
Nordic Spirit Symposium Series History   ***61***

Introduction

Nordic Spirit Symposium at California Lutheran University

Scandinavian Peacemakers and Humanitarians, the topic of this publication, was the 14th in an annual Nordic Spirit Symposium series organized by the Scandinavian American Cultural and Historical Foundation (SACHF) and California Lutheran University in Thousand Oaks, California. This annual series brings a diverse range of Scandinavian topics to the southwestern United States for a two-day program of lectures and performances designed to educate and entertain a broad audience.

The series was conceived in a meeting of the SACHF executive committee with Cal Lutheran's president, Luther Luedtke, and Siri Eliason in the late 1990s. Ms. Eliason, Consul General of Sweden in San Francisco and also chair of Cal Lutheran's Board of Regents at the time, informed the group of a "Humanities West" series of cultural/historical programs offered in San Francisco, which became a model for the SACHF-Cal Lutheran Nordic Spirit Symposium. A grant of support from the Barbro Osher Pro Suecia Foundation made it possible to inaugurate the Nordic Spirit symposium in 2000 with a millennium celebration of the Vikings North Atlantic saga, *The Vikings: Westward Exploration, Expansion and Settlement*. The keynote speaker for this program was Dr. Richard Hall, archaeologist and Deputy Director of the Jorvik Viking Centre in York, England, who gave an overview of Viking activities in England. The Viking theme was continued the next year with a program titled *The Vikings: Eastern Traders, Merchants, Empire Builders and Royal Guards*. Keynote speakers for this program were Dr. Björn Ambrosiani, Project Director of Birka Excavations in Sweden, who spoke about the Birka excavations and also about Birka's contacts with Russia and beyond, and Dr. Evgenij Nosov, head of the Novgorod excavations in Russia, who spoke about the first Scandinavians in northern "Rus." Mats Larsson of Sweden spoke about Viking Age Scandinavian activities in the east basing his information on runestones and other written sources, while Erik Axel Wessberg from Denmark spoke about and demonstrated reconstructed Viking age instruments. Other presentations included the record of Vikings in the east through coin hordes, a dramatic reading of Yngvar's Saga, and a change of pace with a program of folk fiddling.

A wide variety of Scandinavian topics have been examined in subsequent Nordic Spirit programs, with two programs devoted to Scandinavia and Scandinavian resistance during WWII, others treating the topic of Scandinavian immigrants to America, and nationalism in the Nordic countries and the peaceful dissolution of the Swedish-Norwegian union. Nordic explorers are well known for their polar exploration firsts, but they have also excelled in other regions of the globe, as treated in two symposia. These explorer programs included presentations by active contemporary adventurers and explorers, as educator and motivational speaker Liv Arnesen, the first woman in the world to ski solo and unsupported to the South Pole, and the "Baffin Babes," two Norwegian and two Swedish women who skied 80 days in the Arctic, described their preparations and Antarctic and Arctic journeys. The ever-popular Viking Age was brought back for the 2008 and 2009 symposia when sagas, myths and a new look at the Viking Age were treated. The February 2013 topic, *Scandinavian Peacemakers and Humanitarians*, became the basis of this present volume of articles. A program on Iceland, land of fire and ice, is planned for 2015. A complete catalog of the fifteen Nordic Spirit Symposia topics treated to date is given in the Appendix.

Music is an important ingredient in these programs, whether performed by acclaimed Grieg pianist Dorothy Schechter, Norwegian baritone Per Vollestad, Minneapolis–based singer, guitarist and kantele player Diane Jarvi, or New York Swedish-American soprano Elly Erickson and Swedish accompanist Samuel Skonberg with their Nordic tapestry of Scandinavian song, or serenading with bassoon, accordion and piano through Finnish music by Terhi Miikki-Broersma.

Participants are encouraged to share the time-honored spirit of a symposium, blending music, dining and the free exchange of ideas to enhance the pleasure of learning. Time for discussion during session breaks and a symposium dinner are thus highlights of each symposium.

The annual Nordic Spirit symposium is made possible by generous grants from the Barbro Osher Pro Suecia Foundation with additional support from the Norway House Foundation* in San Francisco. Support during the series has also come from the Royal Danish Consulate General in Los Angeles, the Royal Norwegian Consulate General in San Francisco and the Consulates General of Finland and Sweden in Los Angeles.

Howard K. Rockstad

Thousand Oaks, California

*Norway House Foundation is a California non-profit corporation dedicated to honoring the Norwegian seafarers who risked their lives for the Allied cause in World War II. The Norway House Foundation carries out its mission by promoting, encouraging and supporting educational, professional and cultural exchange between Norway and Northern California.

Preface

The Nordic Spirit: Peacemakers provides an interdisciplinary study in which "Nordicism," a set of norms and values, informs the decision-making process in contexts far from Scandinavia. Egalitarianism, mediating conflict, exercising influence in new and novel ways, the prominence of national heroes in shaping the course of history, and the role of international connections play out in the disparate contributions in this volume.

In the first chapter, Ingebritsen explains how and why Scandinavia has found a niche in the "soft power" politics of peace making, human rights, egalitarianism, poverty reduction and sustainability. While not always acting vigilantly, this corner of northern Europe exercises an influence beyond its borders, and "punches above its weight."

Carl Emil Vogt traces the role of the hero in global society. Norwegian explorer and diplomat Fridtjof Nansen was internationally known for crossing Greenland on skis, and expressing the common character of the nation. His efforts led to a peaceful dissolution of the Swedish-Norwegian Union and provided an example of Norway's link to an earlier phase of greatness.

Arland Hultgren documents the role of Nathan Söderblom (1866-1931), Archbishop of Uppsala and recipient of the Nobel Peace Prize in 1920. He worked tirelessly to reconcile competing views of engagement, and through extensive conferences for peace, brought together groups that otherwise would not have been created. His work led to the formation of the World Council of Churches, encouraging cooperation across faith communities.

Eric Einhorn's chapter focuses on the contributions of Folke Bernadotte and Dag Hammarskjöld, two active and effective international mediators during a period of instability and regional conflict. Dag Hammarskjöld lost his life on a mission to the Congo, illustrating the high level of risk faced by international peace-keepers.

Herbert Gooch provides an overview of the legacy of Warren Christopher and Earl Warren, demonstrating that Nordic values not only reside in Scandinavian citizens, but extend to their descendants in the New World. In their life's work, the Nordic spirit has been evident—from international peacekeeping to legal norms, embodying values of equality at a conflict-ridden period in American history.

None of these contributions would have been possible without the teamwork provided by Howard Rockstad, Coordinator of the Annual Nordic Spirit Symposium, colleagues in the Scandinavian American Cultural and Historical Foundation and at California Lutheran University, Thousand Oaks, California and the generous support of the Barbro Osher Pro Suecia Foundation and the Norway House Foundation.

Contributors to the Volume

Christine Ingebritsen, Professor of Scandinavian Studies, University of Washington, Seattle, Washington, Co-Editor, *The Nordic Spirit: Peacemakers.*

Howard Rockstad, Coordinator, Nordic Spirit Symposium, Thousand Oaks, and Co-Editor, *The Nordic Spirit: Peacemakers.*

Carl Emil Vogt, Ph.D., Research Scholar, Oslo, Norway.

Arland Hultgren, Th.D., Professor Emeritus, Luther Seminary, St. Paul, Minnesota.

Eric Einhorn, Ph.D., Professor Emeritus of Political Science, Professor of Scandinavian Studies, University of Massachusetts, Amherst.

Herbert Gooch, Ph.D., Professor of Political Science, California Lutheran University, Thousand Oaks.

The Power of Scandinavia

Christine Ingebritsen
Professor, Scandinavian Studies
University of Washington, Seattle

For many of us, the study of Scandinavia begins at home, with the painted wooden chest inscribed with the family name---a memory of the crossing by sea to the United States---or the legend of a spirited aunt who transcended class and gender boundaries in education or the business world and was undoubtedly a descendant of Vikings. Indeed, the power of Scandinavia can be seen in the number of us who can trace our personal histories back to the old country and who have shaped the way the Northwest, Washington State and the University of Washington have developed.

It was Scandinavians who created the first Nordic Heritage Museum in North America; and organized the department where I hold an academic position with a distinguished team of Scandinavian scholars. The neighborhood of Ballard, where national flags continue to fly, culinary traditions are represented, orders of Viking descendants meet at the Leif Erikson Lodge, and Scandinavian languages are still spoken, reminds us of our own city's ethnic identity. And when I cross Red Square, I recall the memory of former University of Washington President Charles Odegaard [a Norwegian] for which our undergraduate library is named.

This article focuses on the legacy of Scandinavianism. Not just at home—but in the world community. In this article, I wish to turn our attention to Scandinavia's global role and how it ties to our educational mission on the 100th anniversary of our Scandinavian Studies department.

I begin with a focus on key concepts and questions:

Where do the boundaries of Scandinavia begin and end?
What do I mean by "power?"

Then, I will focus on

How Scandinavia makes a difference in the world, and how our interdisciplinary department advances global understanding of Scandinavia's footprint on international society

"Scandinavia" refers to the five northern European states (Denmark, Finland, Iceland, Norway and Sweden) and the three territories of Greenland, the Faroe Islands and Aaland Island. The entire population of this subregion of Europe is only 25 million. Given the small size of this northern corner of Europe, these societies have, by necessity, focused their attention on specific portfolios or tasks in foreign policy making. Whether it be a targeted invasion---or a well-orchestrated mediation process.

Power refers to the capacity to influence. Traditionally, power is associated with economic and military might, amplified by superior technology in a particular moment of time. This type of power can be seen in the Viking Age, Sweden's Great Power period, and in the Winter War and War of Continuation fought between Finland and Russia.

Power also resides in IDEAS and NORMS. Whether it is Viking transport—boats constructed to navigate long sea voyages, and used as housing in the off-season. Or a generous gift to honor peace. Or modeling a specific balance of state regulation of the society and economy. Elimination of poverty at home, and exporting aid to the poorest regions of the world. Providing universal health care to all members of the community. Promotion of equality—across all dimensions of society. Developing the economy so everyone is made better off---not just a minority. Promoting green policies, practices and exports to the world economy. Unique and innovative in technology, governance, economic development, conflict resolution and social policy are all powerful. Underlying these ideas are ideologies and values that express how the world <u>should</u> be governed. These norms are present in the literature, films, and cultural production of northern European societies and captured in the classroom learning of our students.

Thus, what is remarkable about Scandinavia extends beyond traditional measures of power: It is the capacity for Scandinavia to "punch above its weight" in a world, that for Scandinavia, has always been global. Some scholars, such as Anand Yang, suggest that a discussion of Scandinavia's power can and must be brief, since Scandinavia has no power. However, my work, and the research and teaching of my colleagues, counters this particular world view, which is grounded in a traditional, narrowly conceived notion of power—incorporating norms, reputation, and the export of novel ideas to world markets and participation in critical global governance networks (i.e. the Elders).

With this more expansive definition of power, consider how Scandinavia challenges expectations of many, and exercises influence outside its territorial boundaries.

From an early time, Scandinavians were explorers, adventurers and traders. Conditioned by proximity to the sea and scarce resources/short growing seasons, they developed technologies to permit international crossings and rowed long distances to return home with the goods necessary to survive a long winter season.

In light of recent theorizing and historic discoveries, the Vikings and their power are worthy of scholarly reflection for several reasons:

1. **they were early globalizers**
2. **they are an example of how globalization and liberalization are not required to go hand in hand**
3. **historic climate change data reveals favorable temperatures which made these crossings easier to navigate**
4. **early egalitarian values emanated from this critical chapter in Scandinavian history**
5. **to this day, Vikings represent fearlessness and are associated with toughness and tenacity**
6. **they lacked the capacity to promote their prowess in North America and, even though they were first, we are reticent to fully acknowledge Leif Eriksen Day**

These early globalizers benefited from conditions, according to historian Brian Fagan in his book, THE LITTLE ICE AGE, favorable due to a warmer than usual climate. And once fiercely imported goods were brought home, these tended to be divided equally and the Viking women retained the power to leave if things did not go as deemed appropriate (they, by the way held the keys and power over the workings of the farm while their partners were away on sea adventures).

Today's Vikings carry briefcases and Nokia cell phones or invite global leaders to attend the awarding of the Nobel Prize for peace. This is, I would argue, a remarkable transformation from the fear of the fury of the Northmen brought upon Europe in earlier phases of history.

During the Viking Age (793-1066 A.D.), warriors from Scandinavia earned a reputation for brutality. According to an observer of a famous attack (one of many, I might add) along the northeastern coast of England, "pagans from the north came with a naval force to Britain like stinging hornets and spread on all sides…robbed tore and slaughtered not only beasts of burden, sheep and oxen, but even priests and deacons."

In 840 A.D. Vikings launched a series of raids on the European continent. Paris narrowly escaped attack. Vikings occupied both banks of the Seine and were poised and ready. Only after obtaining vast sums of silver did the Vikings move on to hold positions in the French countryside.

Without knowledge of the Northmen, our student's educations might be slighted by omission of these moments in history. Thanks to Terje Leiren's educational work on THE VIKINGS, students are provided with a comprehensive treatment of the historic power of Scandinavia in the world.

And Old Norse experts remind us of the egalitarian norms of Viking society. Even during the Viking Age the division of property was decided according to common principles, rights of women were delineated, and boundaries of appropriate and inappropriate conduct were established in law and custom. For example, when a whale washed ashore on the Icelandic coastline, the community shared this resource, and it provided wealth to everyone in the settlement, not just the individual farmer or fisherman.

<u>Collaboration, and seeking common solutions, is associated with Scandinavian power</u>. A union forged in Kalmar, Sweden in 1397 and ending in 1523 is an example of Scandinavian collaboration. Under the reign of Queen Margaret of Denmark, the Scandinavian monarchs agreed to collaborate. Margaret's son, Erik of Pomerania, was named king of Scandinavia (Denmark, Norway and Sweden). At Kalmar, collaboration included a common defense policy, mutual recognition of outlaws and a pledge to remain unified. Although the Kalmar Union could not be sustained, it was a benchmark of regional cooperation, symbolized by the three crowns.

20th century Scandinavian cooperation included extensive collaboration among regional governments to create a passport union, and free movement of persons—prior to the adoption of similar practices in the European Union.

<u>Peaceful solutions also emanate from Scandinavia</u>—even though the northern European area has not always been at peace. Scandinavian democracy can be traced to the first parliament in Iceland, the Althing. Meeting annually to mediate disputes, the Icelanders were early adopters of democratic practices. And as democratic institutions were consolidated in the 1800s and early 1900s, border disputes were negotiated without resorting to violence. The breakup of the Swedish—Norwegian Union in 1905 occurred without armed conflict or longstanding disputes over territory. And when Iceland broke away from Denmark in 1944, this occurred without conflict. Only in Finland did the creation of a Finnish nation-state lead to an outbreak of civil war. Yet in each instance when Scandinavians relinquished authority to another part of Scandinavia, conflict was

averted.

In the modern era, Scandinavia has led the way in seeking innovative, multilateral solutions and has collectively intervened to strengthen codes of conduct in international politics. Scandinavia has also earned a reputation for acting earlier than larger, more powerful actors in the international community on many environmental and social issues. In the 1800s, for example, Finland established restrictions on its timber industry, an early example of environmental regulation. Finland was also among the first nations in the world to grant the vote to women. In Iceland, the founding of the Red Stocking Party in the 1920s represented the first party in the world devoted to women's issues. The Norwegian parliament (thanks to a relative of Seattle native and Norwegian Brewster Denny) established progressive social legislation for workers and families early in the twentieth century. In the 1930s, the ascendance of the Swedish Social Democrats ushered in an era of progressive social policies under the leadership of Per Albin Hanson. And the desire for equality extended to equal representation in the national legislature as indicated in the 1948 election campaign slogan in Sweden, "without women, no democratic governance."

And according to the most recent world economic forum report, Norway is the most equal country in the world in measures of gender equality.

These moments, in the study of power, can be inspiring to other societies and show the promise for democracy of social inclusion.

During the tense years of the Cold War, Scandinavia was strategically vulnerable, lying directly between Moscow and Washington, D.C. However, these governments consistently implemented innovative diplomatic measures to dissipate conflict between the two opposing blocs. By inviting great power leaders to their capitals as sites for conflict mediation and institution building (Stockholm, Reykjavik and Helsinki), Scandinavia cultivated a global role against superior military powers. And when, in a tense moment, Finland was invited to engage in military consultations with the Soviet Union, a back channel message via Norway to NATO enabled a collective response: "Any military consultations between Finland and the Soviet Union is not inconsequential to NATO." The so-called Finnish Note Crisis reveals the creative uses of neighboring states connections to broker "bullying" between small and larger powers in the international system.

Finland also offered the promise of independence from neighboring rule, and inspired the Baltic peoples in their independence movements. Our students have the opportunity to read and speak Finnish—one of the few campuses endowed with this less frequently taught language. University of Washington students receive linguistic and culture training with Andrew Nestingen; and have the unique opportunity to study Baltic society and languages with area expert Guntis Smidchens. Following the break-up of the Soviet Union, the studies of the Baltics were appropriately and peacefully relocated from Slavic Studies to the Department of Scandinavian Studies.

Scandinavia's global influence is multi-faceted. Prominent individuals, referred to in my work as "norm entrepreneurs," socialized by social democratic values at home, export their expertise to the international community. These norm entrepreneurs include scientists, literary figures, economists, politicians and philosophers whose ideas and influence extend beyond the boundaries of Scandinavia.

One such "norm entrepreneur," notably absent from the Al Gore slide show, is Swedish scientist, Svante Arrhenius. Yet it was Arrhenius who in his 1895 lectures in Stockholm explored the relationship between the influence of CO_2 (carbon dioxide) in the air on the temperature on the ground. He was later awarded the Nobel Prize in Chemistry, but not for his study of what we refer to as "the greenhouse effect," but instead for other important findings. The greenhouse effect was not yet politically salient—nor was the environment a global issue in world politics. Yet his work has and remains pioneering in atmospheric and environmental studies, as University of Washington Professor Richard Gammon reminds us.

Fridtjof Nansen, who lived from 1861-1930, was an international explorer, zoologist, artist and statesman. He is one of Norway's most globally recognized leaders who is famous for skiing across Greenland, documenting vital details of the territory, and later working for recognition of Norway's independence from Sweden. In 1920, Nansen became the Norwegian representative to the League of Nations. He created an innovative way to deal with displaced persons in response to a crisis in Russia. By creating the "Nansen passport" he was responsible for helping 500,000 refugees return to their homeland, and was a recipient of the Nobel Peace Prize in 1922; and later in 1938, the Nansen International Office for Refugees received the Peace Prize.

Other prominent "norm entrepreneurs" from Norway include the first General Secretary of the United Nations, Trygve Lie, the only candidate acceptable both to Washington, D.C. and Moscow. And Gro Harlem Brundtland, Norway's first female Prime Minister; who headed the World Health Organization elevating attention to the health of women and children and who now serves as the UN Climate Change Officer. Each of these individuals export ideas from social democratic Norway to the world community.

Across the border in Sweden, there has been a long-standing record of mediating conflict and serving as an example of how to resist developing nuclear weapons, even when the technology is readily available. Sweden has been the most generous of all welfare states in levels of social spending, and institutional innovations. It was the first to formally create the office of the Ombudsman, designed to mediate between the individual citizen and the government, an office widely adopted by many universities and public institutions—including the University of Washington. To understand the Swedes, we turn to two colleagues, Lotta Gavel-Adams and Ia Dubois, who chair the Swedish Studies Program and have been honored by Sweden for one of the leading programs in the world.

Nobel Peace Prize winner, Martti Ahtisaari, is another example of how Scandinavia exports its norms of international cooperation to the global community. His diplomatic engagement extends from Europe to Asia and Africa, and he has played a role in mediating ethnic, religious and racial divisions—most recently in Iraq. Working for peace and reconciliation has won him the prize which each year is awarded on the anniversary of the death of Swedish industrialist and peace broker, Alfred Nobel, December 11th.

The study of norms is also central to our teaching and learning in literature and cultural studies. Norwegianists Jan Sjavik and Katherine Hansen remind us of the power of Ibsen. Henrik Ibsen documented class and gender dynamics in Norwegian society, drawing attention to inequalities. Marianne Stecher-Hansen focuses our attention on Danish history and society and the ways literature promotes a particular worldview. Other leading scholars explore how Scandinavian crime fiction is a window on new tensions in these societies. Visiting scholars and lecturers (including Jan Nielsen from Denmark, and Anna Ronnko from Finland) are funded by Scandinavian governments to be in residence at US academic institutions and keep our learning environment actively engaged around questions of power. Herein lies our educational legacy and role 100 years beyond the establishment of the Scandinavian language requirement through an act of the Washington State legislature.

If we move away from place, and consider the collective influence of Scandinavia, we have yet another facet of Scandinavia's footprint and legacy.

SOFT POWER IN FOUR DISTINCT ISSUE-AREAS

In four distinct issue-areas, Scandinavian institutional and policy choices have shaped the expectations of policy makers who represent these societies in external negotiations. Even though there have been profound changes within the political systems of Scandinavia, the legacy of past choices and political priorities continues to guide Scandinavian foreign policy makers. In international relations, small does not mean ineffective when it comes to Scandinavia: administrative flexibility and the capacity to mobilize limited resources efficiently has given smaller states a comparative advantage in critical areas of decision making.

The Retention of Universalism

Even though Scandinavian societies are becoming more multicultural and welfare reform is more pressing than welfare expansion, Scandinavia remains the ONLY group of states that continues to provide assistance to all residents of the society—citizens and non-citizens. This model has not been exported to other parts of the world, but is historically unique to the Scandinavian area. And these societies are far from adopting British, American or Continental systems of welfare provision.

The underlying norm within Scandinavia is equality. Everyone should be treated in the same manner, as a basic right in these societies. There is also a strong sense of responsibility for the collective group. From an early age, Scandinavian students work in teams on collective projects, and later in the workforce, collaboration also plays a vital role as indicated by innovative team-based manufacturing in leading companies such as Sweden's Volvo production lines.

Scandinavians have been socialized to expect a particular active role for the state. Thus, the legacy of universalism, and the institutional and policy innovations of decades of social democracy persist. When Scandinavians go abroad, they are quick to point out how things might work differently.

With more Scandinavian societies joining the European Union, there has, for example, been a new voice at the table. Sweden has actively pursued policies to promote equality, and the Danes have introduced ways to make decision-making more fair and provide citizens with an equal voice.

Another legacy of Scandinavian exceptionalism is the preference for conflict avoidance—visible in virtually every dimension of daily life—but also a prominent "niche" for these states in a period when common security is deemed more appropriate than territorial security.

Conflict Resolution and the Promotion of Peace

At home, Scandinavia has a legacy of forging bargains between actors that traditionally have been at odds with one another. Two such historic bargains are frequently the subject of study in our political science coursework: the labor peace agreements (labor withholds the power of the strike in return for a say in the process of wage negotiations and working conditions) and the Cow Deal between farmers and social democrats that provided a political base for the ideas of Scandinavia's innovative version of capitalist democracy. The Farmers Party promised to support the Social Democratic Party in return for agricultural subsidies and protections.

The Scandinavian norm of conflict avoidance has translated into innovative peace-keeping and peace-making efforts in world politics. For example, the combination of reassurance and deterrence policies so as not to aggravate security relations between east and west during the cold war is particularly novel. As the European Union forges a common foreign and security policy, Scandinavian governments advocate non-traditional forms of preserving security, documented in the Amsterdam Treaty's Petersburg Tasks. The capacity for Scandinavians to forge agreements, mediate conflict and to act as an international broker for peace stems from societal norms that are deeply held.

Even in our own departmental meetings in Scandinavian Studies, peace and conflict avoidance prevail. All hard decisions are taken in the corridors prior to the meeting to avoid unnecessary confrontation.

Harnessing Technology for Social Purposes

Another area where Scandinavia plays a powerful role is in the acquisition and uses of technology. Scandinavia has been described as a "digital Valhalla" referring to how these societies exercise global leadership in cell-phone technology. Ericsson of Sweden and Nokia of Finland are two leading cell phone companies which are market leaders in Europe. These companies consistently challenge producers in larger more economically powerful states in providing global service and in developing e-technologies.

Not only have Scandinavian companies emerged as technological innovators, but they also lead the world in cell phone use per capita. Providing access to new forms of technology to the greatest possible number while also monitoring the health effects of reliance on cell phones distinguishes the cellular age in Scandinavia from other parts of the world. Norms matter as Scandinavians register concern over the consequences of wealth creation among an emergent group of young entrepreneurs; and nationally funded studies have been conducted documenting the physical effects of cell phone use.

Scandinavian governments invest heavily in research and development to retain a competitive hi-tech presence and to innovate for the future. Cooperative arrangements across national borders facilitate greater competitiveness in world markets. According to a vice president from a leading Seattle internet company, "Nokia's success in transitioning from a forestry-based company to a mobile phone exporter depended on sharing technological innovations with Swedish-based Ericsson." As demonstrated by the success of the Scandinavian Airlines System (SAS, a joint company created by Denmark, Sweden and Norway), cross-border economic partnerships have enabled Scandinavian companies to prosper internationally. And as Nokia partners with Microsoft, further innovation and entrepreneurship is anticipated.

Thus, technological entrepreneurship is not limited to the west coast of the United States, but is also found in Europe's northernmost corner where a generation of "e-vikings" are embracing new technologies and harnessing these to improve the economy and the quality of life in these societies.

Since the taming of the Vikings, some would argue that the most powerful aspects of Scandinavia's global role is the legacy of eliminating poverty at home, others would focus on promoting peace and cooperation, or harnessing technology for social purposes. I will argue that Scandinavia's power is on the rise—in matters vital to the planet and the quality of life in a global society: the pursuit of sustainability within and outside the Scandinavian area. And eco-leadership depends on everything else Scandinavia has represented: the transformative effects of the welfare state, trust in government, reliance on new technologies, and harnessing these through national and collective partnerships.

SCANDINAVIA AND THE GLOBAL ENVIRONMENT

Scandinavia is emerging as a more important player in world politics today precisely because of its early and consistent management of natural resources. The term "sustainability" captures what has long been a Scandinavian practice of long-term restrictions on growth and development designed to insure the prosperity of future generations. This is evidenced by Finnish forestry management practices dating to the late 1800s; Norway's decision to restrict oil and gas production and to save revenue for all of society in a privately invested Petroleum Fund; Sweden's active role in cleaning up the Baltic Sea; Iceland's fisheries management system; and Danish innovations in land reform and green agriculture.

Two principles are central to Scandinavian environmental norms which also frame the context of decision making outside the region. The rule known as *allemannsrett* which refers to the access of all members of society to natural areas; and the tradition of protecting the environment for recreation or "friluftsliv" are fundamental codes of Scandinavian social interaction.

It is thus not surprising that Denmark has become the home of the European Environmental Institute. Danish court cases brought before the European Court of Justice (the subject of Professor Rachel Cichowski's new book) have significantly advanced sustainable practices particularly in the area of recycled products. The labeling process adopted by the Nordic Council with the image of a swan designating to consumers and industry products which are "environmentally friendly," can and should be a model to other societies and to the EU.

As colleague Annica Kronsell argues, the Swedes have cultivated a niche within European policy making as leaders in advancing more stringent collective measures to protect the environment. This is particularly evident in the adoption of rules governing the use of chemicals in Europe. The legitimacy of these states, as early and relatively clean industrializers, places Scandinavia in a unique position of advocacy and legitimacy in this vital area of global collaboration and regime building.

We could not think of a better group of advisors in the UN—in the offices of conflict mediation and climate change than the prominent Norwegians who have been exported to fill these tasks: Jan Egeland and Gro Harlem Brundtland.

How Does Scandinavian Studies Connect Young Scholars to the Study of Power?

Through the role of literature, politics and society, students grasp the importance of ecology which captures Scandinavian eco-entrepreneurship and leadership in the greening of capitalism.

What Other Projects Reflect the Priorities of Our Teaching and Learning?

Heather Short explores how and why nostalgia is so powerful to Norwegians. Peter Leonard analyzes Swedishness in a society where what it means to be Swedish is evolving. In her dissertation entitled, "Its Raining Men," Mia Spangenberg traces the effects on masculinity of changes in women's power in Finland. Mark Safstrom reflects on the role of religion as an extension of state power.

WHAT'S HOT IN COLD STATE STUDIES?

Greenlanders are pursuing greater autonomy from Denmark. A protectorate of Denmark since 1721, the 56,000 residents of Greenland may opt for independence from Danish rule due to economic benefits from global warming. Greenland is a site for ecotourism, due to the warming of the climate and the calving of the glaciers. Cod fishing has improved, broccoli and potatoes can be cultivated, and lead, zinc, gold and diamonds are increasingly abundant and accessible due to retreating glaciers.

Iceland has received global attention equivalent to the era of the Cod Wars with Britain. The banking crisis reminds everyone in the global community of the dangers of unregulated, overly zealous bankers seeking profits with new financial instruments. Thanks to international institutions, Iceland has been rescued, yet significant diplomatic repair is needed with Britain, whose PM Gordon Brown treated Icelanders as terrorists. Troubling as it may seem, Iceland has relied on its dependence on norms to shame Britain for bullying, and seek to turn the table on its more powerful neighbor. Unwilling to see Icelanders suffer, the Faroe Islands announced short-term transfer of resources to assist the economy and society until IMF funds can be fully secured.

As more immigrants comprise Scandinavian populations, what will be the response? Assimilation, integration, multiculturalism? Scandinavia has traditionally had strong social norms of conformity: how flexible will these societies adapt to diversity, and what policy options are the most promising? What will the role of Scandinavia be in seeking equality and human rights among those who do not share the common social democratic ethos and rituals of the north?

Not all norm entrepreneurs emanate from Scandinavia. There are ways in which others are influenced by norms, yet may not have ever traveled to Scandinavia. The extension of Scandinavian ideas could, for example, influence Washington State (as the Governor and

Seattle mayor go green), and also shape the array of policy options in national capitals around the globe.

As the global banking crisis continues to require attention, the lessons of Sweden's response to ailing banks (national control, reregulation, and then privatization) can be contrasted to the role of Japan (where Japanese have been faulted for a slow, deliberate and savings-centered strategy).

When more knowledge of specific innovations in alternative energy are needed, we can call on the Danish firm Vestas to guide T. Boone Pickens in his dream of creating windmill farms in Texas. As we explore whether we can make stadiums sustainable, we only need a few Icelanders to document the benefits of geothermal power. And as mayors seek to implement more and more policies from Scandinavia (bike lanes, reusable bags, advanced recycling techniques), we again experience the soft power of Scandinavia.

And as we reflect upon how our students are trained the preparation for global service is clear: they will be ready for a sustainable future, ready to rely on creative uses of technology and innovation, aware of best practices and the imprint of Scandinavianism, past and present.

We recall the moment in her confirmation hearings when Condoleezza Rice was asked to define the Nordic Council. Small potatoes for our Scandinavian scholars, who could hold a short lecture on the topic.

In Conclusion

Scandinavians have experienced systems of governance with separate and distinct underlying principles, collective expectations, and a clear role for the state in society. In foreign policy making today, we see the legacy of the Scandinavian model playing out in important ways—from preferences for equality and social justice to mediating conflict; working for more stringent environmental standards, to techno-sociological innovations, the Scandinavian experience brings powerful norms and policy legacies to the international community for critical discussion, engagement and adoption.

The educational capacity of universities and colleges has its legacy as well. Our collaborative efforts have forged partnerships with scholars across all fields and disciplines from Bergen to Hong Kong. To regularly welcome visitors from Scandinavian and Baltic societies creates an opportunity to actively engage in a learning community. And with so much power in our Scandinavian community, we continue to rely on the generosity of our friends to strengthen our efforts to explain the Scandinavian way.

This think piece has given a frame to evaluate how Scandinavia exercises its power. These comments do not necessarily reflect the views of colleagues at the University of Washington, but as a political scientist my work has very much been shaped by them.

I have two closing thoughts which I ask you to retain beyond this article: beware of defining power too narrowly: you may just miss the richness and diversity of world politics—past and present.

And beware of delegations from northern Europe: they have an agenda, and they are as determined and tenacious as earlier warriors emanating from this corner of the globe.

Thank you for the honor of presenting this contribution as part of the centennial celebration of the Department of Scandinavian Studies, and as a "Nordic Spirit" program presented at California Lutheran University made possible by the Barbro Osher Pro Suecia Foundation, with additional support from the Norway House Foundation.

Fridtjof Nansen:
From Polar Explorer to Humanitarian Hero

Carl Emil Vogt, Ph.D.
Researcher, The National Library of Norway, Oslo, Norway

Fridtjof Nansen, the Nobel Peace Prize Laureate for 1922, played a major part in building the League of Nations and in leading humanitarian operations in the aftermath of the First World War.[1] He was the League of Nations High Commissioner for Repatriation of Prisoners of War from 1920-22, he led the Red Cross-initiated famine relief to Soviet Russia from 1921-23; and not the least, he became the first High Commissioner for Refugees. He was also a prominent representative in the League of Nations Assembly. Apart from this, however, Nansen was an accomplished scientist, a gifted writer, and an eminent explorer. He also played a role in Norwegian diplomacy, informally in 1905 when Norway gained her full independence of Sweden, and later as the first Norwegian ambassador to London in 1906–08 and later envoy to Washington to negotiate food provisions for neutral Norway during The First World War. As he was a Norwegian national hero, he also became an icon for the internationalists.

Nansen became a candidate for humanitarian leadership for three main reasons, his position as a world famous explorer, his pre-war and wartime diplomatic experience, and the fact that he came from a small neutral country. One could probably also add a fourth dimension, his charisma. He was in several ways a perfect example of what Max Weber has called a charismatic leader.

The Rise of a Hero

Fridtjof Nansen was raised in an upper class family, though not a particularly wealthy one. Both his father's bourgeois and his mother's noble families belonged to the Norwegian élite originating in Denmark and Germany. The young Nansen showed an early interest for skiing in the areas around Kristiania (Oslo). After passing his first exams at the city's University, he saw the Arctic Ocean and the coast of Greenland for the first

---

[1] My article on Nansen as a Nobel Peace Prize Laureate (Vogt 2006) also offers a short biographical sketch and analyses his humanitarian work. A fairly good biography on Nansen is available for an English speaking audience: Huntford 1997. This article draws heavily upon Vogt 2010 and Vogt 2011.

time while on an expedition for the Department of Zoology.² He was given a position as a researcher in Bergen in 1882, and visited experts in Germany, Italy, and Great Britain to learn the newest methods and apply them in his research. Through his scientific training, Nansen established his first international network. His research was actually cutting edge in what we today call neuroscience.

In 1888, after having submitted his doctoral dissertation in zoology, with a small team he went straight on to achieve the first ever crossing of Greenland.

The success was followed by a bold attempt to reach the North Pole, by the means of drifting with the vessel *Fram* (which means *forward* in Norwegian) in the ice more or less over the pole point. Nansen's theory was that strong currents were leading from the coast of Siberia to Greenland. Nansen proved his theory, but Fram did not reach the Pole. It drifted too far south of the Pole. In a futile push, which easily could have cost them their lives, Nansen and a companion left the ship on skis to conquer the North Pole with dogs, kayaks and sledges. They had no hope of returning to the ship and had to make their way to the south after giving up at 86° 14' North, which was the farthest north any man had been to that date. When Nansen in 1896, after three years on the ice, suddenly appeared, almost literally walking off the ice as a survivor, he became an international sensation, received by emperors and prime ministers alike. His book on the expedition became an international best seller, still printed in numerous languages.³

In 1897-98 he visited the United States and Canada with a lecture tour, not the least to finance an expedition for the South Pole. It all went well on the east coast and he attracted great audiences. But Nansen was tired and did not manage to attract the same kind of audiences in the Midwest and in smaller places. In the end the whole tour became a disaster. Nansen broke his contract and was sued by his own American agent; he insulted public audiences and even had a nervous breakdown in St Louis – while speaking in a theatre.⁴ When leaving America, he sounded like a classical anti-American: "...a half-civilized, half developed people, which still has plenty to learn, they lag far behind us", he

---

² The Royal Frederik's University, Norway's only one until the 1940s. Nansen's research position was at Bergen Museum, the nucleus of the University of Bergen when it was established in 1946.
³ For example *Farthest north: the epic adventure of a visionary explorer*, New York 2008; *In Nacht und Eis: die norwegische Polarexpedition 1893–1896*, Stuttgart 2006, *Furamu gô Hokkyoku Kai ōdanki: kita no hate* [Farthest north], Tokyo 1998, *Vers le pôle*, Paris 1996.
⁴ See for instance New York Tribune 7 November 1897: «Dr. Nansen is suffering from a slight attack of nervousness»; New York Times 20 November 1897: «Dr. Nansen's health is giving way under the strain of his lectures and the receptions accorded him everywhere, and he says that in the future he will not take part in any demonstrations»; An article in the New York Times, 30 January 1898, was extremely critical.

wrote to his closest friend the painter Erik Werenskiold.[5] Nansen did not return for 20 years. His failure at this lecture tour was the obvious reason.

In Norway, carried on a wave of strong national sentiment, he was lifted onto a pedestal, and portrayed as a masculine and virile Viking king who could solve the nation's problems. His successful expedition was, both by himself and not the least by others, portrayed as a national triumph. All this made it possible for him to play a major part in the struggle for Norwegian independence from big brother Sweden. In 1905, when the union was peacefully dissolved, the government used him as an agitator at home and a negotiator abroad – especially important in Great Britain. Nansen demonstrated a quite pragmatic and effective understanding of politics in 1905 when first using belligerent rhetoric to achieve the break, then transforming it to moderate and compromising as soon as the secession was a fact (Wiggen 2006). He also agitated for Norway to remain a monarchy despite his private republican leanings – the reason was obvious: the European Great Powers would not accept a Norwegian republic. In 1905 Nansen followed, however, the lead of a shrewd politician, Prime Minister Christian Michelsen, perhaps the only Norwegian politician whose authority he would readily accept. Nansen's political astuteness during this year could partly be a result of Michelsen's strategic thinking.

Being well connected with British upper class circles, even with the royal family, Nansen became Norway's first ambassador to Great Britain 1905–1908, when Norway established her own foreign service. Most importantly he led the negotiations for an integrity treaty with Britain. After having served his country and his government these three years, he withdrew from the political scene, to concentrate on his scientific studies. His position in Norway was more solid than ever. After the death of Bjørnstjerne Bjørnson in 1910, a renowned poet and Nobel laureate as well as political activist, Nansen's position as a national hero was uncontested.[6]

He had built a network of international contacts first as a student, then as an explorer and scientist. He experienced that this network and his position could be used to promote the Norwegian cause abroad; he had become an experienced diplomat and negotiator, but still wanted to pursue a scientific career. However, the growing fear of war pulled him back to the political scene. The Great War was in fact to become the great schism in his thinking, like for so many other European and American intellectuals living through those

---

[5] Nansen to Erik Werenskiold 28 December 1897 in Nansen: *Brev,* vol. II, no. 248.
[6] The only conceivable rival was the 1905 Prime Minister, Christian Michelsen, who had led Norway to independence.

cataclysmic times.

The war brought hard times for Norway, which was extremely dependent on supplies from abroad, food and fuels in particular. In 1917-1918 Nansen was sent as the leader of neutral Norway's delegation to Washington D.C. to seek vital food provisions. There he negotiated with US Food administrator and leader of the Belgian relief operations, Herbert Hoover, and also met with President Woodrow Wilson. Hoover respected Nansen and later wrote (Hoover 1958, 120): "we became friends". He described Nansen as "a fine, rugged character, a man of great moral and physical courage." Nansen closed the food provision deal on Norway's behalf with the US and the Allies earlier than both Sweden and Denmark.

President Wilson's famous 14 points became a turning point. Nansen decided to work for a new world order and saw the idea of a League of Nations as a starting point. In 1919, Nansen went in private capacity to the peace conference in Paris, where he was approached by his acquaintance, Herbert Hoover, who now was in charge of the American relief and reconstruction programs for Europe. Hoover wanted Nansen to head his planned Russian operation (Hoover 1951, 414). Nansen accepted, but to Nansen's great frustration, the plan came to nothing.

Humanitarian Engagement: Prisoners of War

After the League of Nations was founded, however, Nansen was appointed to the first Norwegian delegation in the autumn of 1920 and soon came to hold a prominent position in the Assembly (Cecil 1941, 117). But even before this, in April 1920, he accepted the post as the League's High Commissioner for Prisoners of War (Huntford 1997, 599–609; Housden 2007; Balzter 2004). His task was to bring POWs home, most of whom were located in Russia and Germany.

In the course of only two years, 1920 to 1922, Nansen and the League of Nations succeeded in bringing 430,000 prisoners of war home.[7] About half of them were citizens of the former tsarist Russia who were transported from Germany mostly on ships through the Baltic Sea. From transit camps in the Baltic States, refugees coming from Russia were returned on the same ships to Germany and many further to the Austro-Hungarian successor states. In fact around 80 percent of the refugees returning to the west were from the former Habsburgian states.

---

[7] *League of Nations – Official Journal,* November 1922, Annex 400, pp. 1223–1225.

In addition to the repatriation operation, an organization called *Nansenhilfe*, the Nansen Relief, was set up to send food and clothing to the prisoners of war in Russia, but it never became of great importance (Balzter 2004, 30). The success of the repatriation effort itself, however, was formidable, but it was only made possible through the support of Great Britain and France, Germany, and the Habsburg Empire's successor states (Yugoslavia, Hungary, Czechoslovakia, and Austria). In addition came the support of the Soviet Government.

The Allied powers would not negotiate with the Bolsheviks directly, because they did not recognize what they considered an illegal communist regime. The Great Powers, not least the Soviets, were quite happy with Nansen becoming the leader for repatriation of prisoners of war; so were the most important Non-Governmental Organizations. But first and foremost: Nansen had close ties to the British both through his personal contacts and through League of Nations personnel. Nansen's High Commissioner's office was situated in London. In many ways Nansen was as close as the British could come to having an Englishman in the office (Huntford 1997, 606).

Famine Relief

Nansen's next endeavor was famine relief work in Russia from 1921 to 1923. This time he was the choice of his collaborators from the Prisoners of War work.

Russia was hit by a major crop failure, which threatened to put 20–30 million people into famine conditions. Nansen and his collaborators initially planned to grant Russia large-scale loans to finance food relief.[8] The supplies were to be delivered by an organization operating in Russia on the exact same principles as the *Nansenhilfe*.[9] This included cooperation with the soviet government, which was controversial when it came to relieving starving *Russians* and not Western Prisoners inside the Communist state. Anti-bolshevism proved very strong, and his relief plan was never realized, as the League of Nations refused to take charge of it and only passed the issue on to the Great Powers that refused to grant any credits. Instead, Nansen's operations inside Russia had to be based on a loan from the Soviet government and private donations. In France and Great Britain, support for Nansen's action was scant. Nansen desperately tried to turn the tide by appealing especially to the British public and politicians through a series of lectures in

---

[8] The credits were again to be provided by the International Committee for Relief Credits.
[9] That is: a central distributing Committee in Moscow, with one representative of Nansen's and one from the Soviet Government, local distributing committees with Soviet representation.

sixteen British cities with films and photographs from his own trip to the famine areas. But the plan to grant Russia loans was rejected by the British Parliament in the spring of 1922.

The situation was quite different in the US where by then Secretary of Commerce Herbert Hoover through his semi-official aid agency, the American Relief Administration (ARA), managed to feed at the most 11 million Russians at one and the same time (Patenaude 2002; Weissman 1974; Fisher 1927). The US Congress granted 20 million dollars. Nansen's budget was small, totaling 1.2 million dollars, in comparison with the ARA's more than 60 million.

The European famine relief work had to be organized outside of the League of Nations, although close collaboration with the International Labor Organization (ILO) and the League's Epidemic Commission was established. Nansen and his collaborators had to build an organization from scratch, with great help from the International Committee of the Red Cross (ICRC). But again, no lasting organization was built, as the situation was acute and the operation *ad hoc*. Nansen himself, however, had wanted to turn the relief organization into a more permanent development aid project, but this proved politically impossible, as neither the Soviets nor the West wanted it.[10] His attitude had clearly changed from the POW work that he just had wanted to get on the right track and then get rid of.[11] The hunger relief operation had suffered severe problems, mainly because of lack of money. But yet again the network proved strong and creative; insights were gained and refined from their experiences.

Refugees

Nansen's third humanitarian project concerned refugees. He became the League's first High Commissioner for refugees. Again he proved to be the strongest candidate both because of his experience and his small-state background. Nansen's refugee work began in 1921 and lasted until his death in 1930.

The Russian Revolution, and especially the bloody Civil War (1918–1920), had forced

---

[10] As long as possible (until 1924), Nansen kept a small secretariat in Moscow. Even after that two model farms were run by Nansen, one in Ukraine the other in the Volga area, but in 1927 they were handed over to the Soviet authorities who all along had disliked the project, but the order to stop them had been mislaid in the growing Soviet bureaucracy in 1927, and Nansen's engagement in Russia ended. See the Nansen Archive, Ms. fol. 1988, R6A1, "Agreement with Soviet Russian and Ukrainian authorities of 27 September 1927".

[11] Nansen to Edouard Anton Frick, 24 June 1921 in Nansen: *Brev*, vol. 4, no. 708.

more than one million Russians to flee the country (Skran 1995, 32). The international refugee work was initiated as a response to a growing pressure from European public opinion and the Red Cross. That a concern for the situation increased even in Spain and Belgium, countries without many refugees, suggests a conscious humanitarian public opinion in Europe at the time. Great Britain and France realized the scale of the problem, and wanted the League to handle it (Skran 1995, 289–90). In that way they could distribute the costs to as many other parties as possible.

At first, Nansen's engagement included only Russian refugees (meaning refugees from former tsarist Russia, thus including a wide range of ethnic groups). But his mandate was later to be expanded to other geographical areas. One example is his successful, but already at the time highly contested, plan to exchange Christian refugees from Turkey with Moslems living in Greece (Huntford 1999, Tolleshaug 2001). Today many would call this "ethnic cleansing", but this is not entirely correct. "Ethnic cleansing" involves an actual genocide or mass murder, whereas this operation was clearly a transfer, however brutal it may have been for many of the people involved. Moslems in Greece had to leave their homes for abandoned farms in Turkey. It is, however, necessary to mention that most of the 1.1 million Greek refugees had already left Turkey, following the now retreating Greek army. Greece was the country in Europe with the largest proportion of refugees, 1.4 million or almost 20 per cent of the entire populace. To send Moslems to Turkey seemed the obvious solution at the time (Skran 1995, 41–48). This project was carried out successfully, and large loans were given to the Greek government. The success of Nansen's plan should rather be explained by the fact that the Great Powers supported the plan, and that both Greece and Turkey wanted it, than by pointing at the excellence of the planner.

Another example of Nansen's refugee schemes was his prolonged and deeply felt concern for the fate of the Armenian refugees from the official Turkish genocide policy. Plans were drawn up to build a new home for the refugees in the Soviet Republic of Armenia. Soviet Armenia was to be lifted out of poverty through large-scale irrigation projects. The plan was not supported by the West, and an increasingly Stalinist Soviet Union turned against it. Thus the plan never became a reality although Nansen fought long and fiercely for it.

The refugee work was initially an ad hoc operation like the POW work inside the League of Nations, and the famine relief work outside of the League. But the refugee organization gradually became a more permanent and general institution inside the League. This is mirrored in the changing of the title from High Commissioner for Russian Refugees to High Commissioner for Refugees. During Nansen's period as High Commissioner, even though the office was constantly underfinanced, rules for tackling the refugee problem were established. In addition the pioneering "Nansen Passport" for refugees without citizenship was invented and provided legal rights to hundreds of thousands of refugees (Torpey 2000, 127–129).

From the beginning in 1922 only persons of Russian origin could acquire the passport. In 1924 Armenians were also included. The Nansen Passport was a considerable success. By the end of the 1920s more than 50 governments had recognized the document. The refugee historian Claudena Skran sums up: "The beginning of international refugee law can properly be dated to the creation of the Nansen passport system" (Skran 1995, 105). John Torpey, author of The Invention of the Passport, agrees: The Nansen Passport represented "the first step toward resolving at the supranational level the internal contradictions of a system of movement controls rooted in national membership" (Torpey 2000, 129).

By the end of the 1920s, the future of the High Commissioner's office seemed uncertain. It was hard to plan for a future for the High Commissioner's office, and indeed for the people working in it. Nansen was tired and felt he needed a replacement. The High Commissioner's office was taken into the secretariat of the League of Nations and the British Thomas Lodge was appointed Deputy High Commissioner to help Nansen reduce his commitments as he had asked for. Lodge was chosen and appointed at Nansen's own request, albeit strong opposition since the administrative department of the League's secretariat should have taken the formal decision. Nansen never learned to go through the proper channels, and never wanted to learn it because of his strong dislike of any bureaucracy. Lodge was a close collaborator of Nansen's with the economic responsibility for the POW work, the famine relief operation, and the refugee work.

The refugee regime built up under Nansen in the 1920s gradually collapsed in the 1930s, like the League of Nations itself. The problem with new groups of refugees was not tackled, most prominently Jews from Nazi Germany.

Achievements

So, which were Nansen's humanitarian achievements? They varied of course greatly. My findings are to a significant degree in contrast to most of the existing literature, where his humanitarian work predominantly is presented as a chain of successes. The achievements of the prisoners of war work were indeed formidable; it turned out to be considerably less expensive than expected and 430,000 soldiers were exchanged. The operation strengthened the League of Nations itself. The least successful part of it was the Relief Organization *Nansenhilfe*, Nansen Aid, which never made much of an impact.

The mode of cooperation with the Soviet Government developed with the *Nansenhilfe* was used also in the later aid organization during the famine. This relief operation was not well conducted; the central organization was too weak to coordinate and lead the operation effectively, and the financial system, which also was taken from the on-going prisoners of war operation, never became functional. The propaganda effort of Nansen and his collaborators may, however, have made an impression on European minds. It was one of the first times that pictures and even films, and stories from a famine area in a relatively different culture made its way to the newspapers and lecture halls of Europe. The impact of images of human suffering has often been profound. In addition, the importance of different organizations working under Nansen's auspices, like Save the Children, should not be forgotten. These organizations, and their individual relief workers, also developed their organizational and practical skills during the Russian operation.

When it comes to Nansen's appointment as High Commissioner for Russian Refugees in 1921 and the Nansen passport from 1922, these were in fact the beginnings of international refugee law. They were even among what the Human Rights historian Paul Lauren calls " 'significant new departures' in the development of international human rights" (Lauren 2003, 119). The international refugee regime, which was established, somehow survived the 1930s, and was then reconstituted after the Second World War. The United Nations High Commissioner for Refugees is a grandchild of Nansen's High Commissioner's office from the 1920s. The Refugee historian Claudena Skran concludes: "Although many great names are associated with the League's refugee work, Fridtjof Nansen's strong and creative leadership left a mark on refugee assistance which is still evident today" (Skran 1995, 287). It was however, only his refugee work that has had a lasting legacy in the form of institutions. Both the prisoners of war work and the famine relief work were *ad hoc* operations. But Nansen seems to have moved gradually away from *ad hoc* thinking; it was obvious in his ideas for development of Russia and Armenia. Increasingly, Nansen became a more systematic institution builder. This was, given his initial dislike of bureaucrats, bureaucracies and orderly authority, in fact quite a transformation.

Nansen's room for maneuvering, and indeed that of the League of Nation's or of the

NGOs, was extremely limited, however. When the Great Powers, in particular Great Britain and France, or the other states directly involved, supported his humanitarian projects, then he was given the opportunity to succeed. When the opposite was the case and the states decided against Nansen's plans, very little was achieved. The famine relief project to Soviet Russia failed because the Great Powers, in this context mainly Great Britain and France, decided against it. The repatriation of the prisoners of war, however, became a great success partly because the Great Powers, Germany, the Austrian successor states, and the Soviet leaders wanted it. The Great Powers also needed the Russian refugee problem to be solved. The Greek-Turkish exchange of refugees was a solution accepted by the Great Powers – and Greece and Turkey. Nansen's plan to resolve the Armenian problem, was neither politically supported by the Western Powers nor the Soviet Union, and it came to nothing.

This said, Nansen and his allies creatively exploited the given possibilities. This is a perfect example of "diplomacy as the art of the possible". Being one of the first international civil servants, he was a great entrepreneur who opened the field for later humanitarian actors. But in international relations entrepreneurs rarely succeed without a substantial power base – Nansen and the League lacked both military and financial clout. To sum up: Not very surprisingly, Nansen only succeeded when supported by the Great Powers; his room to maneuver was to a very large degree defined by them. On the other hand, given the extremely tight framework they operated in and their constant lack of resources, Nansen and his collaborators' achievements were impressive.

Nansen was a strong, charismatic, and authoritarian leader, a (former) macho-man and adventurer; as an idealist he could therefore not easily be dismissed as being weak. His fame and position, and the fact that he was acceptable both to Soviet leaders and Western politicians, made him an ideal person to rally behind for internationalists both inside and outside the League of Nations. But behind the issue of his symbolic value lurks the question of to which degree he was an independent agent or controlled by others. It is quite clear that Nansen was not controlled by Norwegian politicians during and after the First World War. He seems to have been fairly independent of the Foreign Service even as a Norwegian delegate to the League of Nations. He was however open to the influence of greater actors like the British, possibly also the Soviets, and he was politically naïve to a certain degree. On the other hand he also had a strong will and ability to improvise, cut through red tape, solve problems, and eventually to build new institutions. And if nothing else is true about Fridtjof Nansen – he definitely achieved a lot by *behaving* as if he represented a Great Power, not a small state. In short, he had transformed from a polar explorer to a humanitarian hero.

Literature:

Balzter, Sebastian 2004. "Repatriierung 1920-1922. Zur Rückführung der Kriegsgefangenen nach dem Ersten Weltkrieg," Magisterarbeit, Freiburg im Breisgau: Albert-Ludwigs-Universität.

Fisher, H.H. (Harold Henry). 1927. *The famine in Soviet Russia 1919–1923. The operations of the American Relief Administration,* New York: Macmillan.

Hoover, Herbert. 1951. *The Memoirs of Herbert Hoover. Years of Adventure 1874–1920.* New York: Macmillan.

Hoover, Herbert. 1958. *The Ordeal of Woodrow Wilson.* New York: McGraw-Hill.

Housden, Martyn. 2007. "When the Baltic Sea was a 'Bridge' for Humanitarian Action: The League of Nations, the Red Cross and the Repatriation of Prisoners of War between Russia and Central Europe, 1920-22", in *Journal of Baltic Studies*, 38 (1), 61–83.

Huntford, Roland. 1999. "Fridtjof Nansen and the Unmixing of Greeks and Turks in 1924", *Nansen memorial lecture 1998*, Oslo: Videnskapsakademiet.

Huntford, Roland. 1997. *Nansen. The Explorer as Hero.* London: Duckworth.

Lauren, Paul Gordon. 2003. *The Evolution of International Human Rights.* Philadelphia: University of Pennsylvania Press.

Patenaude Bertrand M. 2002. *The big show in Bololand: The American Relief Expedition to Soviet Russia in the famine of 1921.* Stanford: Stanford University Press.

Tolleshaug, Berit. 2001. *Fridtjof Nansen. En norsk helt i en gresk tragedie.* Oslo: Pax.

Torpey, John. 2000. *The Invention of the Passport. Surveillance, Citizenship and the State,* Cambridge: Cambridge University Press.

Vogt, Carl Emil. 2002. " 'Et ikke ubetydelig bidrag.' Fridtjof Nansens hjelpearbeid i Russland og Ukraina 1921-1923" with summary in English. in *Forsvarsstudier*, No. 2. Oslo: Norwegian Institute for Defence Studies.

Vogt, Carl Emil. 2011. *Fridtjof Nansen: Mannen og verden.* Oslo: Cappelen Damm.

Vogt, Carl Emil 2006. "Fridtjof Nansen. Peace, 1922," in Olav Njølstad (ed.): *Norwegian Nobel Prize Laureates. From Bjørnson to Kydland*. Oslo: Universitetsforlaget, 119–153.

Vogt, Carl Emil. 2007. *Nansens kamp mot hungersnøden i Russland 1921-23*. Oslo: Aschehoug.

Vogt, Carl Emil. 2010. "Nestekjærlighet som realpolitikk. Fridtjof Nansens humanitære og internasjonale prosjekt 1920-1930" PhD: University of Oslo.

Vogt, Carl Emil. 2008. " 'Our own people first' How the Newspaper Aftenposten sabotaged Nansen's charity to Russia," English summary of article in *Historisk Tidsskrift*, Norway, 87 (1) 2008, 189.

Weissman, Benjamin M. 1974. *Herbert Hoover and Famine Relief to Soviet Russia: 1921-1923*. Stanford: Hoover Institution Press.

Wiggen, Gunnhild. 2006. *Fridtjof Nansen: Taler og artikler fra 1905*. Oslo: Novus.

Peace through Justice and Reconciliation: The Legacy of Nathan Söderblom

Arland J. Hultgren
Luther Seminary
St. Paul, Minnesota

Within the small circle of clergy members who have received the Nobel Peace Prize, Nathan Söderblom was the first (1930). Others in that circle include Martin Luther King, Jr. (1964) and Desmond Tutu (1984),[1] who are much better known. It should probably come as no surprise that Söderblom does not come to mind when one thinks of the Nobel Peace Prize, as the others might, for he was a citizen of a relatively small country (Sweden), devoted most of his work to relationships between churches of Europe that were alienated from one another during World War I and its aftermath, did that a long time ago, and lived and worked prior to coverage of his work by television and its worldwide reach. By contrast, King and Tutu were on the world stage before and after receiving the prize.

Nevertheless, Söderblom was in fact an important and influential thinker and activist in the early part of the twentieth century. Since he is not widely known outside of ecclesiastical circles, a brief sketch of his life and career is in order here at the outset:

- Birth: January 15, 1866, Trönö, Hälsingland Province, son of Pastor Jonas and Sophia Blume Söderblom.
- Graduation *(fil. kand.)*, Uppsala University (Humanities, including ancient languages), 1886.
- Graduation *(teol. kand.)*, Uppsala University (Faculty of Theology), 1892.
- Ordination as a *präst* (priest/pastor) in the Church of Sweden, 1893.
- Marriage to Anna Forsell (1870-1955), 1894. Together they had 12 children (4 daughters, 8 sons).
- Pastor in Paris and Calais, 1894-1901.
- Th.D., Protestant Theological Faculty of the Sorbonne, Paris, 1901.
- Professor at Uppsala University, 1901-1914.

---

[1] In addition to Christian clergy, a good number of other religious leaders and writers have received the Nobel Peace Prize, including Albert Schweitzer (1952), Mother Theresa (1979), Elie Wiesel (1986), the Dalai Lama (1989), and others.

- Concurrently Professor at University of Leipzig, Germany, 1912-1914.
- Archbishop of Uppsala, 1914-1931.
- Convener of the Universal Christian Conference on Life and Work, Stockholm, August 19-30, 1925.
- Death: July 12, 1931.

An additional and interesting detail to add to this sketch is that while Söderblom was pastor of the congregation in Paris, one of his parishioners was Alfred Nobel. They had a significant relationship, since Nobel was interested in discussing theological questions. Later Pastor Söderblom officiated at the memorial service for Nobel in 1897.[2]

This essay consists of five parts: (1) a survey of Nathan Söderblom's career; (2) his major thoughts concerning church unity; (3) a discussion of his views on social issues; (4) the Conference on Life and Work in Stockholm in 1925; and (5) reflections on Söderblom's legacy and some comments on his receiving the Nobel Peace Prize in 1930.

I. The Career of Nathan Söderblom

One cannot grasp the thinking of Nathan Söderblom apart from his deep Christian commitments and his career as a pastor, professor, and archbishop. In connection with his professional roles, he spent significant times abroad, in which he encountered cultures and people different from those at home, and he made life-long friends who affected his thinking and activities throughout his life.

He grew up in a home where his father, a pastor, was an adherent to Lutheran pietism. Söderblom himself had a pietistic conversion experience at the age of twenty-four. But unlike many pietists who were anti-intellectual, he was driven to ever greater adventures of the mind, seeking to understand not only the Christian faith and tradition, but other religious traditions as well.

As a student at Uppsala University, he was particularly gifted in acquiring foreign languages. That included not only modern languages, but ancient as well, including the fundamentals of Avesta Persian,[3] which equipped him for the study of Zoroastrianism years later at the Sorbonne in Paris, and to write his doctoral dissertation there on the concept of the future life in Zoroastrianism.

---

[2] This and other biographical information, when not credited elsewhere, is often drawn from the magisterial and detailed work of Bengt Sundkler, *Nathan Söderblom: His Life and Work* (Lund: Gleerups, 1968).
[3] Ibid., 26.

The breadth of interest in the religions of the world outside of Christianity was unusual for a Lutheran academic in Sweden at that time, and certainly for one who would become the Primate of the Church of Sweden. He taught in the field of "the history of religions" at both Uppsala and Leipzig; the subject is usually called "world religions" in North American colleges and universities.

At the age of twenty-four, while still a student at Uppsala, Söderblom traveled to the United States to attend a conference of the Student Christian Movement, held at Northfield, Massachusetts, in 1890. He remained in New England for two months and discovered the wide variety of religious denominations in the US, and they piqued his curiosity and his appreciation of them. It was there, while living with a family in Connecticut, that he composed a prayer that was in some ways a preface to his later career: "Lord, give me humility and wisdom to serve the great cause of the free unity of Thy Church."[4] That prayer tells something about his leadership in the future, for throughout his career he could not think of the unity of the church other than something into which the various churches would enter freely.

During those years and throughout his career Söderblom affirmed that God is revealed in religious systems outside of Christianity. He sought to gain an understanding of the religions of the world in all their diversity, particularity, and richness. He believed that his calling and duty as a scholar was to investigate what can be observed in the religions of the world, past and present, and interpret them with fairness. Although he held to the superiority of Christianity among the religions of the world, because of its "special" revelation in Christ, for him that had to be held in check when engaged in scholarship. He affirmed that all the major religions of the world have a validity of their own, based on "general" revelation.[5] God, he thought, was a living God, and God's revelation is dynamic through the continuing, evolving development of creation.[6] The reality and holiness of God can be apprehended by people everywhere. Söderblom presented papers on the study of religion at academic conferences at Stockholm, Paris, Basel, Oxford, and Leiden prior to assuming the office of Archbishop.[7]

His years of parish ministry in Paris and his teaching at Leipzig provided opportunities

---

[4] Quoted from ibid., 38.
[5] This is made clear in various publications, and also in his letter to A. C. Headlam, 13 April 1922; copy in the Söderblom Archives, Uppsala.
[6] Derek R. Nelson, "Encountering the World's Religions: Nathan Söderblom and the Concept of Revelation," *dialog: a journal of theology* 46 (2007): 368.
[7] Eric J. Sharpe, "The Legacy of Nathan Söderblom," *International Bulletin of Missionary Research* 12/2 (April 1988): 66-67.

to gain friends in both France and Germany and to know both French and German cultures prior to World War I. He had life-long friends in both of those countries, as well as in England, Scotland, the United States, and elsewhere. That had importance for his work in seeking peace among the combatants during and after the war.

Söderblom was appointed Archbishop of Uppsala on May 20, 1914, three months before the outbreak of World War I in August. His first act as Archbishop in September of that year was to prepare and publish in seven languages an appeal to the churches of the world entitled "Peace and Christian Fellowship." To gain support, he acquired the signatures of leaders of churches in the Nordic countries, Switzerland, the Netherlands, and the United States to accompany his own. In spite of his efforts, however, he was not successful in obtaining the signatures of any leaders in the countries actually at war, including the UK, France, and Germany.[8] The appeal contained a simple message, calling upon all who have influence to keep peace in order that bloodshed might cease.[9] But war had already commenced, and the appeal was not heeded by the leaders addressed by it. Then in 1917 Söderblom hosted a conference of churches at Uppsala from neutral countries where the main ideas were worked out for what was to become the Life and Work movement, founded in 1920.[10] All together, Söderblom led church leaders, primarily of Scandinavia, in three wartime peace appeals.[11]

A sketch of Söderblom's life and influence would hardly be complete without reference to his interest in the Swedish emigrants to North America. Söderblom had an uncle and a brother living in California,[12] and he often wondered how the Swedes who migrated to America fared. He had a particular interest too in the Swedish branch of the Lutheran Church in North America known as the Augustana Lutheran Church (a predecessor body of what is now known as the Evangelical Lutheran Church in America), and which he himself regarded as the "daughter" of the Church of Sweden.[13] In order to demonstrate his affection for that church, he invited it to send a representative to his consecration as Archbishop of Uppsala in 1914. The Rev. Dr. Lars Gustaf Abrahamson went, and he

---

[8] B. Sundkler, *Nathan Söderblom*, 163-64.

[9] Wolfram Weiss, "Irenic Mediator for Unity—Partisan Advocate for Truth: Nathan Söderblom's Initiatives for Peace and Justice," in *Nathan Söderblom as a European*, ed. Sam Dahlgren (Uppsala: Church of Sweden Research Department, 1992), 16.

[10] Ibid., 18.

[11] E. Theodore Bachmann, "Ecumenical Movement," in *The Encyclopedia of the Lutheran Church*, ed. Julius Bodensieck, 3 vols. (Philadelphia: Fortress Press, 1965), 1.757.

[12] B. Sundkler, *Nathan Söderblom*, 37, 303.

[13] Nathan Söderblom, *Från Upsala till Rock Island: En Predikofärd i Nya Världen* (Stockholm: Svenska kyrkans diakonistyrelses bokförlag, 1925), 346.

participated in the laying on of hands at the request of Söderblom himself.

Then in 1923 the Augustana Lutheran Church received Nathan Söderblom as a guest, accompanied by his wife Anna. The two were in the United States from late September until early December of that year. During that time he preached in two dozen Augustana congregations from coast to coast, and he gave lectures not only at major universities, including Harvard, Yale, Chicago, and the University of California, Berkeley, but also at Augustana Theological Seminary, Rock Island, Illinois (now, due to a series of mergers with other seminaries, called the Lutheran School of Theology at Chicago), Gustavus Adolphus College, St. Peter, Minnesota, and Luther Junior College at Wahoo, Nebraska.[14] The sheer force of his personality made a huge hit with many. In addition, people could sense his warm and heartfelt feelings for Augustana. Among major events in the life of the Augustana Lutheran Church were Söderblom's participation in the dedication of the new buildings of Augustana Theological Seminary in Rock Island on November 6, 1923, and his participation on the same day in the installation of the President of the Augustana Church, the Rev. Gustaf A. Brandelle, in the seminary chapel, including the ceremonial laying on of hands in the rite of installation. Whatever else one might want to make of that, the act at least testified to Söderblom's sense of the deep and historic bond between the two churches.[15] But probably the most lasting effect of Söderblom's visit was a renewed interest within Augustana in its relationship to the Church of Sweden and its theologians, who were making a major, global impact. He also promoted a more positive ecumenical viewpoint in the Augustana Lutheran Church. But spending those months in the United States had an effect on Söderblom too. He discovered the importance of denominations,

---

[14] The itinerary is published in ibid., 380-87. Although his travels in North America and reception by the Augustana Church were not without controversy, both within that church and among its critics outside, he made a huge impact on the synod. On controversy within the Augustana Church, cf. G. Everett Arden, *Augustana Heritage: A History of the Augustana Lutheran Church* (Rock Island: Augustana Book Concern, 1963), 317; for an example of criticism from outside, cf. Mark A. Granquist, "The Augustana Synod and the Missouri Synod," *Lutheran Quarterly* 24 (2010): 48-49. A record of his more endearing presence (including an account of his impact by Conrad Bergendoff) is provided by John E. Norton, "The Archbishop and Augustana," *Augustana Heritage Newsletter* 5/1 (Fall 2006): 13-15.

[15] The event is reported by G. Everett Arden, *The School of the Prophets: The Background and History of Augustana Theological Seminary 1860-1960* (Rock Island: Augustana Theological Seminary, 1960), 220-21. The laying on of hands is related by the archbishop's wife, Anna Söderblom, *En Amerikabok* (Stockholm: Svenska kyrkans diakonistyrelses bokförlag, 1925), 159. She wrote the following: "The laying on of hands during the Lord's Prayer is a beautiful symbol of the connection in time, whether one may pay attention to apostolic succession or not. This solemn installation of the Augustana Synod President, when the Archbishop of Sweden participated in the laying on of hands, became an expression for an even closer connection between the old church in Sweden and the Swedish church body in America" (translation mine).

free of national ties, for the sake of "an inclusive ecumenical strategy."[16]

Söderblom collected his various sermons and lectures and had them published in a volume called *Från Upsala till Rock Island* (*From Upsala to Rock Island*).[17] His wife Anna wrote her own account of their travels in a book called *En Amerikabok*.[18]

II. Nathan Söderblom on Church Unity and World Peace

Söderblom was devoted to peace primarily through church unity, holding the view that all Christians should act together as if they were one body, in spite of divisions, for the sake of healing the social problems of the world and achieving higher moral standards in politics and society.[19] For him, peace can be achieved only by means of justice and reconciliation among nations, and that is an urgent matter. Moreover, he thought, the churches have an essential role to play, and they can take up that role if they will only put differences aside and act together. As he put it on one occasion: "On the Last Day there will be no question of the Articles of doctrine, however important and essential they may be, but of the acts of Love."[20]

Söderblom lived at a time when state and national churches dominated the ecclesial map of Europe. Then too North America's religious scene was dominated primarily by churches of European origin, and they had considerable impact upon public opinion through the various media at a level of importance difficult to comprehend in the present. Today, when reporting on churches and religious leaders, newspapers and other media are more interested in scandals, so it is hard for us to realize that early in the twentieth century, and even well up to the middle of that century, newspapers in the United States were genuinely interested in the life of the church, theological trends, and what major preachers and teachers of the church were saying. Preachers like Harry Emerson Fosdick at Riverside Church in Manhattan and theologians like Reinhold Niebuhr at Union Theological Seminary, New York, were regularly quoted in *The New York Times* and elsewhere. In 1948 Niebuhr was on the front cover of *Time* magazine, and the

---

[16] Carl F. Hallencreutz, "The American Influence on Nathan Söderblom and the Legacy of His Ecumenical Strategy," *Svensk Missionstidskrift* 85/1 (1997): 19.

[17] Cf. note 13 for bibliographical details. "Upsala" (the older spelling of Uppsala) is used in the title of the book and in the writings of Söderblom in general.

[18] For bibliographical details, see note 15.

[19] Nathan Söderblom, *Christian Fellowship or The United Life and Work of Christendom* (New York: Fleming H. Revel Company, 1923), 206-12.

[20] Nathan Söderblom, *The Church and Peace*, Burge Memorial Lecture (Oxford: Clarendon Press, 1929), 25.

Swiss theologian Karl Barth was on the cover in 1962. Their thought was considered provocative and significant for the future of the church and society.[21] The mainline churches were a force for shaping public opinion on the issues of the day.

In the case of Söderblom, he was particularly aware of his role as Archbishop of Uppsala. He made the point that the episcopacy of the Church of Sweden was universally accepted as having preserved an unbroken apostolic succession, giving it a distinctive role within global Lutheranism.[22] For him, the office of bishop in the Church of Sweden stands independent from the state; and it had always been understood that its influence is to extend beyond the national church. He thought of himself as a servant of the church as a whole,[23] and he thought of the Church of Sweden as having a unique role in the work of reconciliation.[24]

Söderblom believed that the churches of the world need some form of unity if they were to speak to the issues of the day. But how? In one of his major writings from 1923, called *Christian Fellowship*, Söderblom outlined three models for unity among Christians. The first is the model of absorption. That is the Roman Catholic model, in which all other denominations would give up their identity and be absorbed by the Roman Catholic Church. But that, said Söderblom, will not work, for it leaves no room for other spiritual homes, and it has no chance of success.[25] The second model is the model of faith, in which there would be agreement among the churches concerning the essentials of the Christian faith, including matters of doctrine and the ordering of ministries. But that too has problems. As he put it, that method "makes too much of formulas and institutions."[26] It would involve endless negotiations and a lot of time. The third model is the model of love, in which there is cooperation among the churches; it is practical, rather than theoretical.[27] That method makes it possible for Christians of widely differing denominations to join

---

[21] To be sure, other religious leaders have been written about in *Time*, particularly those who were the "Man/Person of the Year," including Pope John Paul XXIII (1962), Martin Luther King, Jr. (1963), Pope John II (1994), and Pope Francis (2013). But the articles are more retrospective, looking back on what the persons have accomplished.

[22] Explicitly stated in a letter of January 12, 1931, to an Anglican bishop (Lord Bishop of Gloucester); copy in the Söderblom Archives, Uppsala; also expressed in N. Söderblom, *Christian Fellowship*, 126, where he quotes from the Church Ordinance of 1571, authored by Laurentius Petri, the first Lutheran archbishop of Uppsala..

[23] N. Söderblom, *Christian Fellowship*, 128.

[24] B. Sundkler, *Nathan Söderblom*, 266.

[25] N. Söderblom, *Christian Fellowship*, 122.

[26] Ibid., 155.

[27] Ibid.

together in common ecumenical tasks for the sake of the world.[28] That, he claimed, is the one that can work. It was that model that achieved practical expression in the Stockholm Conference of 1925, of which more will be said below.

The second model that Söderblom spoke of—the model of faith—was actually well under way by 1923. A bishop of the Episcopal Church in the U.S., Charles Brent (1862-1929), had conceived of the movement called Faith and Order. It was organized at Geneva in 1920, but its first official assembly was not held until 1927 at Lausanne, Switzerland.

Although some suggested that the two organizations—'Life and Work' and 'Faith and Order,' both founded in 1920—should hold joint conferences, Söderblom opposed that. He maintained that it is in the practical work of Life and Work that people could get to know one another, trust one another, and then—when that had been accomplished—speak with one another about doctrine and church order.[29] He made the saying famous: "Doctrine divides, service unites."[30] Although logically it makes sense that agreement in matters of faith should precede working together, "psychologically and in the world of reality," he said, "that order is unsuitable and impossible."[31] The church cannot postpone works of love until matters of faith and order are resolved.

III. Söderblom's Views on Social Issues

The thought and convictions of Söderblom concerning social problems can be traced back to his student days at Uppsala. He had grown up in a time when there was increasing alienation of the working class from the Church of Sweden. The clergy and leading lay persons were perceived as being indifferent to the concerns of the labor movement and poverty. As a student at Uppsala the young Söderblom was involved in discussions about the rising importance of the Social Democrats and wrote an article concerning them in a student publication. He asked: "What is the reason for the hostile attitude of the working classes, of the Social Democrats, towards Church and Christianity?"[32]

---

[28] Charles Curtis, *Söderblom: Ecumenical Pioneer* (Minneapolis: Augsburg Publishing House, 1967), 100.
[29] N. Söderblom, *The Church and Peace*, 31-33.
[30] Quijote in a letter of 1922, which is printed in Charles S. Macfarland, *Steps Toward the World Council: Origins of the Ecumenical Movement as Expressed in the Universal Christian Conference for Life and Work* (New York: Fleming H. Revell Company, 1938), 110, and cited by N. Söderblom, *The Church and Peace*, 32. According to B. Sundkler, *Nathan Söderblom*, 340, the phrase had been used already by Hermann P. Kapler in an address at Hälsingborg in 1922.
[31] N. Söderblom, *The Church and Peace*, 38.
[32] Quoted from the essay by Sam Dahlgren, "Nathan Söderblom and the Social Questions," in *Nathan Söderblom as a European*, ed. Sam Dahlgren (Uppsala: Church of Sweden Research Department, 1992), 63.

His thinking was advanced during his years of ministry in Paris and Calais. The congregation in Paris was made up of a wide socio-economic spectrum. There were the well-to-do, such as business men, but also a lot of domestic servants and laborers in factories, who were often unemployed and/or transient.[33] At Calais he was in charge of the mission to sailors. In those places of ministry he faced problems that needed resolution within a just order.[34] In a pastoral report in 1897, he said that his work among the many poor Swedish people in Paris took up most of his time.[35]

As Archbishop, Söderblom was not affiliated with any political party, but he was sympathetic toward the less fortunate in society and was keenly aware of the needs in the fields of employment, housing, and economic justice. He supported the labor movement in particular, including the formation of labor unions.[36] Needless to say, he received lots of criticism from some of the more conservative newspapers.[37]

In one of his works, *The Church and Peace* of 1929, Söderblom declares that the sphere of the church is not politics but the spiritual life. Nevertheless, he goes on to say that human life cannot be split into two spheres. To leave politics and economics to themselves would entail a betrayal of Christianity. He draws upon both the biblical and classical Greek traditions to argue that law and the state are the work of God. But too often the state is deified. Therefore there must be a legal system that embraces all nations. Peace among the nations depends upon law and justice. In the same publication he endorses the League of Nations, although he acknowledges its weaknesses.[38]

Söderblom spoke often about disarmament,[39] and suggested that there be a "supernational commonwealth" which could take the form of a "United States of Europe—without customs offices, frontiers, fortresses and national armaments."[40] In his Nobel speech of 1930 he went so far as to say that a supranational legal system would be a continuation of God's creation.[41]

All of this was rooted in his view of humanity, his anthropology. For him, the root

---

[33] B. Sundkler, *Nathan Söderblom*, 40-41.
[34] Charles Curtis, "Söderblom: Ecumenical Churchman and Theologian," *Christian Century* 83/2 (January 12, 1966): 47-48.
[35] S. Dahlgren, "Nathan Söderblom and the Social Questions," 64.
[36] Ibid., 68-69.
[37] B. Sundkler, *Nathan Söderblom*, 122-24.
[38] N. Söderblom, *The Church and Peace*, 5-11.
[39] Ibid., 15; Nathan Söderblom, "The Role of the Church in Promoting Peace," in *Nobel Lectures: Peace, 1926-1950*, ed. Frederick W. Haberman (Amsterdam: Elsevier Publishing Company, 1972), 115.
[40] N. Söderblom, *The Church and Peace*, 15.
[41] N. Söderblom, "The Role of the Church in Promoting Peace," 101.

causes of humanity's problems can be traced essentially to greed and nationalism. It is for this reason that Söderblom remained steadfast in his insistence that there has to be a renewal in human hearts. Peace can be achieved, he said, only by "fighting against the ancient Adam in ourselves and in others."[42] And "all efforts toward peace should begin in our own hearts."[43] To understand him, one has to be aware of his basic bearings from the Swedish Lutheran pietism of his upbringing.

IV. Conference on Life and Work, Stockholm, 1925

Of all the activities and events that Söderblom arranged, the most important was the Universal Christian Conference on Life and Work in the city of Stockholm in 1925. It was attended by over 600 delegates from 37 countries and 31 churches. It opened on August 19, 1925, and lasted for 9 days.[44]

Given as he was to pageantry and grandeur, Söderblom planned the conference in detail. One of his most outstanding feats was that he had been able to include and invite representatives of the Eastern Orthodox Churches. But equally significant he was able to persuade German, French, and British representatives to attend in a time when feelings of enmity still ran deep between Germany and the other two nations.

Concerning the conference itself, it was a tremendous success on all fronts. Stockholm was festive. People were enlisted from all walks of life to host the conference, including persons who never thought of themselves as concerned with the church.[45] Söderblom had already been in office for a decade and consequently had many contacts in the church and government to get things done. He liked style and flair. In his role as archbishop he had revived the use of colorful vestments. As one of his biographers has said, "As archbishop, Söderblom was always surrounded by an atmosphere of celebration."[46] He had an eye for detail and an ear for music fitting for the occasion.[47] An eye-witness reporter describes the events in this way:

> It was a gathering full of the pageantry which captures the eye. The stately

---

[42] Ibid., 93; and *The Church and Peace*, 26.
[43] N. Söderblom, "The Role of the Church in Promoting Peace," 115.
[44] B. Sundkler, *Nathan Söderblom*, 364-66.
[45] Ibid., 369.
[46] Eric J. Sharpe, *Nathan Söderblom and the Study of Religion* (Chapel Hill: University of North Carolina Press, 1990), 173.
[47] Ibid., 143-44, 366-73.

processional in the cathedral, the brilliant reception by the king and the queen in the royal palace, the…glittering banquet when… twenty-five hundred people were guests of the city…in the magnificent town hall—these and many another events gave a kind of purple richness to the conference. All that grace,…dignity and graciousness could do to give the gathering a noble setting was done by the king, the people and the city. It was rather remarkable to see the crown prince at almost every session of the conference listening intently to all the addresses. The patriarchs from oriental churches gave a touch of remote and baffling color to the scene. And as the days wore on they seemed more and more at home with [delegates from] the West.[48]

The purpose and agenda for the conference had been set in 1922. It was decided that invitations would be sent "to all Christian communions," including the Roman Catholic Church. But unfortunately that church declined the invitation.

Six areas were decided upon for deliberation. They had to do with (1) the church's obligation to be involved in the world in view of God's purpose for it; (2) economic and industrial problems; (3) social and moral problems; (4) international relations; (5) education in the churches concerning the relationships of classes and groups; and (6) models of cooperation among the churches.[49]

One of the major outcomes of the Conference was the sending out to the world its "Message" which began with a statement of the need for the churches to gain new courage for the future.[50] It goes on to speak of various spheres. In the economic realm, the individual person should not be subordinate to industry. Industry should not be based solely on the desire for profit but also be conducted for service to the community. Property ownership involves a stewardship for which one is accountable. Capital and labor must cooperate rather than be in conflict. Other statements have to do with education, concerns of women, and the needs of children. Most direct is the statement on war and peace:

> We summon the Churches to share with us our sense of the horror of war and of its futility as a means of settling international disputes, and to pray and work for the fulfillment of the promise that under the scepter of the Prince of Peace…

---

[48] Lynn H. Hough, "The Conference in Stockholm," *Christian Century* 42/30 (September 24, 1925): 1176.
[49] C. Macfarland, *Steps Toward the World Council*, 104-06.
[50] Portions of the "Message" are printed in ibid., 107-09, and in Michael Kinnamon and Brian E. Cope, eds. *The Ecumenical Movement: An Anthology of Key Texts and Voices* (Grand Rapids: Wm. B. Eerdmans, 1997), 265-66.

righteousness and peace shall kiss each other.[51]

V. The Place of Söderblom in History

The first and most notable legacy of Nathan Söderblom is that he is known as "the architect of the ecumenical movement of the twentieth century."[52] Bishop Eivind Berggrav of Oslo, a contemporary, said that Söderblom was "the creator, organizer and leader of the oecumenical movement."[53] His crowning achievement as a leader was the Stockholm Conference in 1925. Without that event, it is hard to imagine that the World Council of Churches would have come into being in 1948 when Life and Work and Faith and Order merged. Life and Work did more than any other organization to achieve ecumenical cooperation, because it was practical in orientation. The Stockholm Conference on Life and Work initiated unity simply by bringing so many church leaders together, which Faith and Order could not hope to match. The World Council of Churches continues in our day with 349 churches in 110 countries as members. It has a number of units that carry on the concerns of both Faith and Order and Life and Work.

Second, also of ecumenical importance, Söderblom was aggressive in his time to establish full communion between the Church of Sweden and the Church of England, which was accomplished in 1922. He also strengthened ties among the Nordic and Baltic churches. Those initiatives laid the foundation of the Porvoo Declaration that became official in 1994, which establishes full communion among Lutheran and Anglican churches of Scandinavia, the Baltic countries, and the British Isles.[54] It has been said that there is a "remarkable continuity between what Söderblom had in mind" and the Porvoo Declaration.[55]

Third, Söderblom desired already in the 1920s to establish an Ecumenical Institute in

---

[51] Quoted from M. Kinnamon and B. Cope, *The Ecumenical Movement*, 266.
[52] F. W. Haberman, ed. *Nobel Lectures: Peace, 1926-1950*, 121.
[53] Quoted from Peter Katz, *Nathan Söderblom: A Prophet of Christian Unity with Selections from the Memorial Writings of Bishop Berggrav, Bishop Brilioth, Bishop Andrae and Other, and an Introduction by the Bishop of Chichester* (London: James Clarke and Company, 1949), 23. Berggrav was quoting, in agreement, with Arthur Engberg, editor of a Stockholm newspaper (obituary of 1931).
[54] For the text of the Porvoo Declaration, plus background essays, see *Together in Mission and Ministry: The Porvoo Common Statement with Essays on Church and Ministry in Northern Europe* (London: Church House Publishing, 1993).
[55] According to C. Hallencreutz, "The American Influence on Nathan Söderblom," 22, the Porvoo Declaration reflects "continuity" with the thinking of Söderblom.

Geneva.⁵⁶ That hope was finally established by the World Council of Churches in 1948. The Ecumenical Institute opened that year at Bossey, Switzerland, just outside Geneva. To this day the Ecumenical Institute is host to students and researchers from around the world to engage in studies in the fields of ecumenical history and theology, missiology, peace studies, and social ethics.

Finally, the path of peacemaking and reconciliation, so important to Söderblom, remains a hope to be trod. While one cannot draw lines of direct influence from Söderblom to later efforts, his passion for bringing people together to face issues that divide them in open and honest conversation, and then to seek reconciliation among them lives on. One of the most obvious examples is another archbishop, Desmund Tutu, Nobel Peace Prize recipient in 1984, who was one of those who organized the Truth and Reconciliation Commission in South Africa in 1995. At least twenty such commissions now exist in various parts of the world. There is a likeness between the two archbishops in at least one respect. Like Nathan Söderblom, Desmund Tutu has interpreted the office of an archbishop to be, in part at least, a bold leader in the public sphere, taking a stand for human rights and seeking to improve human conditions; and in doing that, Tutu—like the Nobel laureate of Uppsala before him—has considered that a part of his spiritual, pastoral ministry.

Söderblom was a child of his age, but was ahead of his time. His work among the combatants of World War I and his efforts to achieve Christian unity were the principal bases for the Nobel Committee to grant him the Peace Prize in 1930.

In making the presentation in Oslo that year, Ludwig Mowinckel, Prime Minister of Norway and a member of the Nobel Committee, said this:

> Archbishop Söderblom's great achievement is that he has thrown the power of the spirit into the fight for peace. A holder of high ecclesiastical office, he understands the enormous importance of the church in the fight, the powerful influence which it can bring to bear. The Christian church…has a unique opportunity now of creating that new attitude of mind which is necessary if peace between nations is to be a reality.⁵⁷

Then Prime Minister Mowinckel concluded with an optimism that, from the vantage point of today, seems incredible. He said:

---

[56] B. Sundkler, *Nathan Söderblom*, 393-400.
[57] Ludwig Mowinckel, "Presentation," *Nobel Lectures: Peace, 1926-1950*, 77.

> If a new war threatens, the churches will not, this time, bless the guns. They will halt the nations in the name of Him who called Himself the Prince of Peace. At least they say this and commit themselves to it.[58]

That was spoken in 1930. Before long, the politics of Europe changed; the making of armaments flourished; genocide emerged like never before in the history of humankind; and war engulfed nations around the globe.

Will the apostles of peace ever see their dreams fulfilled? Will the prophets who denounce greed, excessive nationalism, and war finally be heeded? We cannot predict the future, but it is people like Nathan Söderblom who give us hope and inspiration.

---

[58] Ibid. Actually Jesus nowhere calls himself "the Prince of Peace" in the gospels. The only biblical writer to use the phrase is the prophet Isaiah (9:6). Nevertheless, Christians have considered the words of the prophet to be fulfilled by Jesus.

From Neutrality to Peacemaking.
The Dangerous Challenges of Mediation:
Folke Bernadotte and Dag Hammarskjöld

Eric S. Einhorn
University of Massachusetts, Amherst

In few regions of the globe has "peace" in the abstract been as central to foreign policy discourse as in the Nordic area. It is not surprising that one of Stockholm's oldest (18th Century) and finest restaurants in Gamla Stan is called "Den Gylene Freden" ("The Golden Peace"). By the 18th Century, Denmark and Sweden had ceased to be significant European powers, and their international status was further reduced in the 19th Century. While both countries would face future threats and conflicts, by 1900 non-involvement and neutrality in international conflicts became the primary foreign policy goal. When Norway and Finland became independent states in 1905 and 1917 respectively, they also pursued neutrality with mixed results. What the Nordic states learned over the past century was that peace and conflict resolution could not rest merely on good intentions and fond hopes. Neutrality and non-alignment were not sufficient in a world of ever wider and more destructive conflicts. Active participation in international politics and even risk-taking would become a key element of their peace policies.

Peace and peacemaking contain several elements in the Nordic context. First, for more than a century the Nordic states have sought to resolve international conflicts through diplomacy, mediation, and arbitration. Over the decades, a "Nordic Way" has evolved for dealing with conflicts and crises. What Christine Ingebritsen calls "norm entrepreneurs" has become a widely accepted concept in Scandinavia. Success, however, is never guaranteed.[59]

Secondly a series of Scandinavian diplomats and statesmen sought to promote the peace resolution of international conflicts and to protect civilians and the victims of war through humanitarian efforts. In recent years Scandinavian military and civilian operatives have swelled their ranks. They have demonstrated great personal courage and creativity, and they have often paid a high price.[60]

---

[59] Christine Ingebritsen, 2002, "Norm Entrepreneurs; Scandinavia's Role in World Politics," *Cooperation and Conflict;* vol. 37 no. 1, (March), pp. 11-23 develops this concept.

[60] A good summary of Nordic foreign policies is Christine Ingebritsen, 2006. *Scandinavia in World*

Thirdly these commitments to diplomacy and conflict resolution have impelled the Nordic countries into the mainstream of international politics, particularly since the end of World War II. Their earlier "passive neutrality" has given way to more proactive foreign policies. Although a common Nordic foreign policy has never been a reality, the Nordic countries share common goals, attitudes, and institutions. This was captured well in the concept of "Nordic Balance," which described an informal but recurring element of due regard for each other's interests and security.[61]

This essay views the origins of Nordic "peace" policy. It is only a passing glance at complex events and developments. I will discuss two major figures from mid-20th

Century Swedish humanitarian and peace mediating diplomacy. They were avatars of Sweden's evolution from low profile neutrality prior to and during the first half of World War II to a more active stance in the last two years of the war and in the postwar world. The two Swedish statesmen are Count Folke Bernadotte and Dag Hammarskjöld. Much has been written about both statesmen, especially Hammarskjöld who courageously sought to expand the role of the UN Secretary Generalship. Not surprisingly both men attracted considerable controversy during their time in action. Both men died violently while pursuing their international mandates. Folke Bernadotte was assassinated in 1948 and Hammarskjöld died in a plane crash in 1961 the causes of which remain controversial.

Historically the older Scandinavian states, Denmark and Sweden, were scarcely pacifistic. They fought frequently with their neighbors and especially with each other. By the 18th Century both had been greatly reduced in power and their belligerence subsided. This era of peace and neutrality was ended during the Napoleonic era. After 1814 Sweden accepted a further reduced role in European politics by with its loss of Finland to the Russian Empire. Despite a crisis in 1815 between Sweden and Norwegian leaders seeking to restore Norwegian sovereignty, war was avoided when Sweden allowed Norway to become a semi-autonomous state under the Swedish crown. Denmark suffered more from bad diplomacy and bad luck: Norway was gone, its economy in ruins, and its power further reduced. Denmark would seek to keep its two duchies Schleswig and Holstein through force in 1848 and 1864. The first attempt was mainly successful, in part because of successful operation of the so-called "Concert of Europe," (support from Britain,

---

Politics. Lanham, MD: Rowman and Littlefield. See also Eric S. Einhorn and John Logue, 2011, "Scandinavia: Still the Middle Way?" in *Europe Today*, 4th ed. Edited by Ronald Tiersky and Erik Jones. (Lanham, MD: Rowman and Littlefield), pp. 191-205.
[61] The best discussion of "Nordic Balance" during the Cold War remains Arne O. Brundtland, 1966, "Nordisk balans før og nå," *Internasjonal Politikk*: 1966:5, pp. 491-541. .

Russia, and France) while 1864 was another diplomatic, military, and political disaster for Denmark as Prussia and Austria seized both duchies. Thereafter military instruments lost much of their attractiveness.

Although Sweden had supported their Danish neighbor – an historical first -- in the mid-19th century confrontations with rising German nationalism and power, there was no direct Swedish military combat commitment. Individual military personnel volunteered to serve with Danish forces (as they would do nearly a century later to aid Finland against the Soviet Union in 1939-40). Swedish troops were dispatched to serve as "peacekeepers" between Danish and German forces, but after 1864 Denmark confronted German power without credible allies. Sweden's main concern was to reduce Russian power in the Baltic which led to increasing sympathy for growing German military power.

Norway had no independent foreign or security policy until full independence was achieved in 1905. Indeed, the reason the Nobel Peace prize was "outsourced" to a committee chosen by the Norwegian parliament was Norway's non-participation in foreign affairs when the peace prize was created by Alfred Nobel. Norway was determined to follow a policy of neutrality as an independent kingdom. Together with Sweden and Denmark, Norway avoided direct participation in World War I. More than the other two countries, however, Norway suffered mainly German attacks on its ships as sea warfare became "unrestricted" as the war progressed.

From these experiences there emerged a Nordic perspective on international relations. Generally the common lesson learned was that wars are rarely successful. Moreover small countries like the Scandinavian have a real stake not only in "peace" in the abstract but in promoting the peaceful settlement of disputes. This was symbolized by Alfred Nobel's creation of the Peace Prize in 1895 (first awarded in 1901). In practice all the Scandinavian countries remained neutral during World War I although Finland, as a Russian Duchy was affected by the war indirectly and even more so by the Russian Revolution. Neutral countries were not fully spared but compared to the belligerents, their losses were modest.

All of the Nordic countries joined the League of Nations despite risks to their common policy of neutrality. They were consistent supporters of international organizations. Twice during the interwar period intra-Nordic disputes were settled by reliance on international organizations: the status of the Åland Islands (Sweden and Finland) and the status of eastern Greenland (Denmark and Norway). While neither involved critical national interests, both generated considerable political heat at the time.

In the wake of World War I Scandinavian humanitarianism became an important element of their foreign relations. The role of the Norwegian explorer and statesman Fridjof Nansen in aiding refugees was a visible example. Despite the role of individual activists and organizations, the Nordic countries still kept a relatively low profile even as members of the League of Nations. Individual acts such as Sweden's gracious transfer of its seat on the League Council to Germany in 1926 as well as Nordic efforts to coordinate the smaller European powers in the early 1930s (the so-called Oslo powers) were among the modest initiatives.[62]

As the political situation in Europe deteriorated during the 1930s, the Nordic countries soon returned to their passive neutrality of an earlier era. Their concern was to avoid the increasingly likely European conflicts, and especially to stay out of the line of fire of Nazi Germany and Soviet Russia. Their implicit commitment under the League's "collective security" provisions was now seen as a potential danger rather than a security guarantee.[63] As we know, only Sweden was successful and at times her position was quite precarious.

Years ago when a young American asked a Swedish diplomat the classic question, "why was Sweden neutral during World War II," he replied ironically and concisely, "because we weren't bombed at Pearl Harbor." The point was that the US remained a "non-belligerent" (with important exceptions) until the Axis powers declared war on it in December 1941, 27 months after the start of the European war. Neutrality in most war requires careful maneuvering by the neutral state and forbearance by the belligerents. Between 1914 and 1918 the Scandinavian states were fortunate; in 1939-40 their luck ran out. Swedish neutrality went through several stages, the details of which are complex. Like other neutrals, not least the USA until 1941, Swedish neutrality policy included whatever maneuvers and concessions that its government felt would keep it out of the war. What is important is that Sweden's flexible neutrality made possible its humanitarian assistance mainly during the final two years of the war.[64]

Sweden was criticized not least by Denmark and Norway for its acceptance of certain

---

[62] Swedish Foreign Minister and politician Östen Undén influenced Swedish foreign policy and diplomacy for 40 years. He served as foreign minister from 1924-1926 and from 1945 to 1961. His role in the reconciliation efforts of the 1920s is discussed by Erik Lönnroth, 1963, "Sweden: the Diplomacy of Östen Undén," in *The Diplomats: 1919-39"* edited by Gordon A. Craig and Felix Gilbert (New York: Atheneum), pp. 86-99.
[63] Under the Covenant of the Leagues of Nations, members states were committed to various "collective security" actions ranging from economic sanctions to direct military action. The inability of the League to mobilize support for collective security contributed to its decline. Rarely has its successor organization, the United Nations, been able to enforce collective security.
[64] See Sverker Åström, 1989, "Swedish Neutrality: Credibility Through Commitment and Consistency," in *The Committed Neutral; Sweden's Foreign Policy,* edited by Bengt Sundelius (Boulder, CO: Westview Press), esp. pp. 21-2.

German military demands in 1940-42, mainly the transit of German military to and from Norway. The western Allies were unhappy about Swedish trade with Germany in raw materials and industrial products, although some very limited trade continued with Britain. Many Swedish diplomats and businessmen had contacts in Germany, occasionally with some very unsavory characters. Overall, however, the mass of Swedish opinion from the royal court to the ordinary citizen was anti-Nazi and anti-Soviet.

Sweden became a haven for Norwegian and Danish resistance fighters and some political refugees, although the numbers were modest until after 1943. As Swedish sources confirmed the Nazi atrocities in the occupied countries against Jews and other targeted groups, restrictions on refugees were gradually eased. More than half of Norway's small Jewish population was able to flee to Sweden in 1941-42. The reception of thousands of Danish Jews in autumn 1943 was a dramatic turning point. Sweden helped to make this remarkable action possible both by spreading warnings of the impending German action again Danish Jews and assisting the refugees in their flight to Sweden.[65]

Sweden's decision to become proactive in humanitarian relief reached a peak in the last months of the war. As German forces retreated from the Red Army in the east and the Allies in the west, they remained solidly in place in Norway and Denmark. German retreat in the very north of Finland and Norway had been devastating to the local population. Sweden feared that Scandinavia could become the final theater of the European War. Moreover, by 1943 it was clear even to the least observant that the Nazi genocide against Jews and others had reached mammoth proportions, including west Europeans and Scandinavians as well. Any targeted populations that did not escape or was not rescued would perish.

More than a few Swedish diplomats, humanitarian organizations and active citizens pressured their government to do more. Swedish businessman and diplomat Raoul Wallenberg's coordination of efforts to save Hungarian Jews in 1944-45 has received much if often inaccurate international attention. Count Folke Bernadotte was second only to Raoul Wallenberg in personifying this effort.[66]

Sweden's shift to accepting refugees was in contrast to its closed borders to most political refugees prior to the war. Danish and Norwegian refugees were accepted discreetly after

---

[65] There are several accounts of the rescue of the Danish Jews. The most is recent is Bo Lidegaard, 2013, *Countrymen* (New York: Alfred Knopf).
[66] For a solid study of the evolution of Sweden's policies during World War II see Stephen Koblik, 1988, *The Stones Cry Out: Sweden's Response to the Persecution of the Jews, 1933-1945*, (New Yorik: Holocaust Library).

1940, including a unit of the Danish army that had actually crossed over to Sweden at the time of the German invasion of Denmark on April 9, 1940. They were repatriated to Denmark when hostilities between Denmark and Germany quickly ceased. Although typical of most European countries (as well as the United States), the highly restrictive refugee policies led to various national policies and international conventions that eased the path for asylum-seekers and refugees in the postwar period.[67]

Folke Bernadotte

Count Folke Bernadotte of Wisborg was the nephew of King Gustav V. Born in 1895, he enjoyed a typical elite upbringing and education and became a cavalry officer, a career with limited possibilities in the army of a 20th C. neutral country. His interest in scouting and later the Red Cross channeled his intelligence and energy into much more productive channels. He married an American heiress, Estelle Manville, and thus had both the financial and personal resources to maintain a wide range of contacts across Europe and North America, including some minor representative diplomatic missions.

During World War II Folke Bernadotte earned considerable good will in both Germany and among the western Allies by arranging POW exchanges. Hence when friends, political figures and especially Norwegian diplomat Niels Christian Ditleff urged him to seek a way of rescuing Scandinavian prisoners in German concentration camps, he was able to establish contacts with several high-ranking Nazi leaders. Heinrich Himmler, the feared head of the SS and the Gestapo, was second to none in his fanaticism and ruthlessness, but by late 1944 he was less deluded as to the likely outcome of the war. Seeking to save his own neck he was willing to risk Hitler's wrath by making overtures to the western Allies for a partial German surrender. Moreover he was open to persuasion by some acquaintances to meet with Count Bernadotte about the Scandinavian prisoners.

After intricate maneuvers with both valiant activists in Scandinavia and some shady characters in Germany, Bernadotte led the organization of several humanitarian rescue operations starting in March 1945 that transported prisoners from several German concentration camps to hospitals and refugee centers in Sweden. Known as the "White

---

[67] At the end of World War II, a controversial group were civilian and military refugees from the Baltic states that had made it to Sweden. Civilians were granted asylum, but in 1946 Sweden sent about 150 Balts who had served in German military units back to the Soviet Union. This became a *cause celebre* as described in Per Olof Enquist's 1968 novel *Legionärerna: en dokumentroman [The Legionnaires: a Documentary Novel]*. In 1994 Sweden apologized to the surviving "Legionnaires."

Busses" Bernadotte's convoys transported thousands of survivors, many of whom were in desperate condition, up through war-torn Germany into Denmark, which was still under German occupation, and on to Sweden. The busses were painted white with large red crosses, Swedish flags, and other markings. They were accompanied and supported by other vehicles, supply stations, and several hundred Scandinavian volunteers. Despite the markings, several vehicles were attacked by allied aircraft who did not know of the mission. Fortunately casualties were few.[68]

Particularly prisoners in the Neuengamme (near Hamburg), Ravensbruck, and even Theriesienstadt camps were rescued. About 21,000 prisoners were rescued in March, April and early May 1945, of whom 8,000 were Danes and Norwegians, nearly 6,000 Poles, 2600 French (mainly women), and even 1124 German prisoners. In these operations an estimated 1615 were Jews. Obviously this was only a "lucky handful" compared to the numerous victims who perished earlier or were beyond the range of the "White Buses."

Even after Germany's surrender the White Busses continued their mission and another 10,000 prisoners were rescued. Early accounts claimed that Bernadotte had promised Himmler to neglect Jewish prisoners, but there is no evidence for this. Of the approximately 31,000 prisoners Bernadotte and his colleagues saved, some 6,500-10,000 were Jews. What is remarkable was that Bernadotte and his staff were able to work with an assortment of German war criminals who had led the massive concentration and death campus complexes. For years after the war there were conflicting accounts about the rescue operation but the fact that more than 30,000 lives were saved makes it one of the few bright points in a very grim history.[69]

After the war, Bernadotte continued his humanitarian and organizational work. In May 1948 he was soon persuaded to undertake another mission, no less challenging than the rescue mission of 1945. He sought to mediate implementation of various UN proposals to end the conflict between the new state of Israel and its Arab neighbors. His title was "United Nations Mediator in Palestine."

Bernadotte's Last Mission

---

[68] Bernadotte's own account appeared just after the end of World War II. Folke Bernadotte, 1945, *The Curtain Falls; Last Days of the Third Reich*. (translated by Eric Lewenhaupt). (New York: Knopf). A more objective and detailed study is by Swedish historian, Sune Persson, 2000, "Folke Bernadotte and the White Buses, " *Holocaust Studies: a Journal of Culture and History,* vol. 9, no. 2-3 (Autumn/Winter), pp. 237-268.

[69] Persson, *op.cit.* discusses and debunks much of the "disinformation" about Bernadotte and the rescue missions.

The events leading to the partition of the British "Mandate" of Palestine is long and convoluted. Having essentially promised the same territory to two different people, the British sought to contain the growing conflict between Palestine's Arab and Jewish populations while minimizing their burdens. The events of World War II – the Holocaust as well the formation of a Jewish brigade in the British Army – strengthened the Zionist position both in the mandate and internationally. That some key leading elements of the local Arab population sided with the Axis reduced their influence. Jewish emigration to the British "Mandate" of Palestine increased dramatically at the end of World War II as few Jewish survivors of the holocaust wished to remain in eastern or central Europe. Britain's various efforts to find a stable future for Palestine faced growing resistance from both the Jewish/Zionist population and the Arab population of Palestine as well as opposition from the increasingly assertive Arab states of the Middle East. With the Labour Government in London winding down the British Empire, there was little appetite for continuing the administration in Palestine in the face of violent and costly resistance.

The UN tried to "mediate" a settlement based on partition of Palestine that satisfied neither the Arabs nor many of the Jewish residents. In May 1948 the Jews unilaterally declared the independence of the State of Israel. Immediately it was attacked by all of its Arab neighbors. Folke Bernadotte and his staff, now including the American diplomat Ralph Bunche, sought to stabilize the various cease-fires and armistices that were arranged. Bernadotte followed the UN plan of partition toward a "two-state solution" made more viable by an economic union, various transit and access rights, and an international status for Jerusalem and its environs.

While mainstream Israeli leaders were still willing to accept some compromise, there were on both sides groups that rejected any compromise. In the wake of several Arab military defeats, some Arab leaders, particularly King Abdullah of Jordan, were willing to consider compromises. The radical Zionists saw partition as a threat to their maximalist demands. In September 1948 the extremist "LEHI" known also as the Stern Gang plotted an assassination of Bernadotte and his top staff. On Sept. 17, 1948 Folke Bernadotte and his aid, French Colonel Serot, were shot at close range. All of the perpetrators escaped, and none were ever punished despite strong expressions of regret from the top leadership of the new Israeli government. Indeed one of the plotters, Yitzhak Shamir, would later become Prime Minister in the 1980s.[70]

---

[70] The embarrassment of Israeli officials at the terrorist operations of the "Stern Gang" may have contributed to efforts by some supporters of Israel to denigrate or cloud Bernadotte's role in the 1945 rescue missions in Germany. Even 60 years later, the assassination is controversial in Israel. See Donald

UN Mediator Ralph Bunche would eventually work out a tentative armistice based mainly on the battle lines of 1948-9. Unsolved would be the future status of Jerusalem, the fate of the refugees, and the recognition of Israel by its Arab neighbors. Following recurrent incidents and three major military campaigns in 1956, 1967 and 1973, many of the issues on Folke Bernadotte's agenda remain unresolved.

Dag Hammarskjöld 1905-1961

Dag Hammarskjöld is widely remembered today as the most successful Secretary-General of the UN, a post he held from 1953 until his tragic death in 1961.

Hammarskjöld became Secretary-General because his predecessor, the Norwegian statesman Trygvi Lie (Labor party Foreign Minister in exile government) had become too controversial in the wake of the cold war.[71] Norway and Denmark had in 1948 abandoned their traditional non-aligned neutrality in favor of NATO membership. Their modest contributions to the UN action in Korea 1950-53 further irritated Stalin's Soviet Union. It may not be entirely coincidental that Hammarskjöld was approved as the 2nd UN Secretary-General less than a month after Stalin's death.

Hammarskjöld's background was exceptionally broad. Trained first in the humanities, he also completed degrees in law and economics. He had become a professional economist working for the Swedish Riksbank (Central bank) and then for the wartime all-party coalition government. He was a "technocrat," not a partisan, but he believed strongly in the "planned economy."[72]

A Swedish civil servant was acceptable to all of the UN Security Council's Permanent Members[73]. At the time there were in fact only two traditional "neutrals" left in Europe: Sweden and Switzerland and the Swiss would not join the UN for several decades. The emerging "non-aligned" caucus of "Third World" countries symbolized by India and other newly independent countries had not yet taken full form.

Macintyre, "Israel's Forgotten Hero: the assassination of Count Bernadotte and the death of peace," *The Independent*, 18 September 2008. http://www.independent.co.uk/news/world/middle-east/israels-forgotten-hero-the-assassination-of-count-bernadotte--and-the-death-of-peace-934094.html

[71] Trygve Lie's style established the precedent for an activist UN Secretary-General, but also the likely political consequences of activism. Lie and his supporters were displeased with Hammarskjold's willingness to replace Lie. See. Roger Lipsey, 2013, *Hammarskjold; a Life*, (Ann Arbor, MI: University of Michigan Press), ch. 5, esp. pp. 95-97.

[72] For details of Hammarskjold's life prior to and during his UN service see *Ibid.* and Brian Urquhart, 1972, *Hammarkjold*. (NY: Knopf).

[73] In 1953 the UN Security Council consisted of nine members, five "Permanent Members" (China – Taiwan at the time, France, the Soviet Union, United Kingdom, and the USA) each of which has a "veto."

Hammarskjöld demonstrated his style early in his tenure: cautious, discreet, self-effacing yet strongly committed to the UN, to the interests of the smaller powers, and creative. His motto was "Quiet Diplomacy." In 1954-55 he produced his first major breakthrough when he visited Beijing, China (not a UN member[74]) and negotiated the release of 15 American airmen held prisoner in China after the Korean Armistice of 1953.

One of Dag Hammarskjöld's most creative innovations occurred during the Suez Crisis of 1956 when Israel, Great Britain and France intervened in Egypt in response to various provocations. Together with Canada's Foreign Minister Lester Pearson, Dag Hammarskjöld proposed a United Nations Emergency Force (UNEF) as a beefed-up truce supervision corps and buffer between the belligerents. Hammarskjöld and Pearson could rally Swedish and Canadian forces quickly, and they were soon supplemented by units from the other Scandinavian countries, Latin America, Asia and elsewhere. UNEF managed the withdrawal of British and French forces, and gradually the Israelis withdrew to the armistice lines of 1949. With UN assistance the Suez Canal reopened several months later under Egyptian control.

This model of a UN military force to act as "peacekeepers" worked well in the Middle East until 1967, when Egypt and its allies again threatened Israel and ordered the UNEF to withdraw from the Sinai peninsula. With the UNEF buffer forces gone and Egyptian blockade of Israel's only Red Sea port, Israel felt compelled to initiate military action with enormous consequences for the Middle East to this day. UNEF had been peacekeepers and truce observers but had neither the mandate nor capability to "enforce" peace.

That challenge arose in 1960-61 in central Africa where the "winds of change" were sweeping out remaining colonial regimes. Shortly after gaining independence the former Belgian Congo descended into chaos during the summer of 1960 and provoked outside intervention. A deadlocked UN, with Soviet hostility to the UN and Hammarskjöld rapidly increasing, could barely act. The phrase "leave it to Dag" had become both a sign of his competence and creativity (to those who supported him) and a symbol of UN paralysis. Again a military peacekeeping force was cobbled together "ONUC" (French acronym) with non-aligned but initially heavily Scandinavia composition.

> It was in connection with these more assertive "peacemaking" goals, keeping the Congo together against secessionist forces and outside intervention (East and West), that Hammarskjöld undertook his fatal last mission. En route to negotiations in

---

[74] The Chinese "seat" was occupied by the Republic of China government on Taiwan until 1971.

Northern Rhodesia (now Zambia), Hammarskjöld's DC-6 aircraft crashed killing the Secretary-General and all passengers and crew. Whether this event was an accident or sabotage remains a matter of controversy to the present.[75]

By the time of his death the very nature of the UN Secretary-General was under challenge mainly from the Soviet Union but from other quarters too. UN activism had filled an important void but had only tenuous political support. Although Hammarskjöld had been easily re-elected in 1957, his activism and effectiveness had cost him support. His successors have varied in quality and energy but none could command the respect and effectiveness of Dag Hammarskjöld.

From Passive Neutrality to Active non-alignment

Both Bernadotte and Hammarskjöld encouraged a new role for the Scandinavian countries, especially Sweden. Although Sweden did not follow her western neighbors into either the World War II alliance or later NATO, she increasingly sought a role as a mediator, facilitator and even advocate for conflict resolution. More than elsewhere in Scandinavia, Sweden was increasingly attracted to "neutralism" and honorary status in the Third World.[76] By the 1970s under the more controversial leadership of Olof Palme, Sweden challenged both the American and Soviet hegemony in various international controversies. Cessation of nuclear testing, nuclear proliferation, apartheid in South Africa, intervention and revolution in Latin America became issues in which Sweden voiced strong opinions if rarely decisive influence.

With the end of the Cold War in 1989-91, the issue of Non-alignment was reassessed in Sweden as in the other European "neutrals." No longer was membership in the European Union thought incompatible with non-alignment. Sweden followed Finland and Austria into the EU, but like Denmark, it maintained several "opt-outs." The efforts of Swedish

---

[75] The investigation by UN and Rhodesian officals (Northern Rhodesia was under colonial rule in 1961; it is now the country of Zambia) was problematic. A recent study presents some evidence that sabotage or an attack by hostile aircraft may have caused the crash, but none of the evidence is conclusive. See Willams, A. Susan, 2011, *Who Killed Dag Hammarskjold?: The UN, Cold War, and White Supremacy in Africa*, (New York: Columbia University Press).

[76] Early in the Cold War pacifist and leftist political forces in Scandinavia argued for non-alignment and criticism of the two blocs, though mainly the US and its European allies. See I. William Zartman, 1954, "Neutralism and Neutrality in Scandinavia," *The Western Political Quarterly*, vol. 7, no. 2 (June), pp. 125-160. As the process of decolonization spread through Asia and Africa, the concept of the "Third World" spread. Only the non-aligned but authoritarian Communist state of Yugoslavia gained full acceptance to this loose bloc.

diplomats to end the Balkan wars in former Yugoslavia were only partially successful. Sweden gave significant economic support to the "post-communist" regimes in Europe, especially the Baltic states. Sweden would also contribute to continuing UN supported peace-making efforts including a modest but symbolically significant role in Afghanistan after 2001. The recurring issue of membership in the expanded North Atlantic Treaty Organization (NATO) was discussed at length but Sweden (along with the other neutrals) decided against membership.

Sweden's international profile has been more restrained during the past two decades as the country copes with economic challenges and social changes. It remains active in a myriad of international organizations contributing personnel as well as political and economic support. Sweden remains a refuge for the global waves of immigrants and refugees despite the rise of substantial domestic skepticism about the viability of these liberal policies. While the mid-twentieth century events that motivated Bernadotte and Hammarskjöld are distant, their legacy remains.

The 20th Century demonstrated that few countries could escape the impact of international conflicts, but that there were several paths to effective foreign and security policy even for smaller powers. Staying out of conflict is still a goal, but passive isolationism is no longer an instrument of choice. Building on the "peace-making" goals of Nobel, Nansen, and later Bernadotte and Hammarskjöld has provided a constructive alternative. The development of European and global commitments to human rights, peace-making, and peace-keeping were spurred by the actions of these two Swedish statesmen.

The tradition of diplomatic mediation, quiet diplomacy and creative institution building would be taken up by other Scandinavian statesmen both in national governments and international organizations. Similar contributions would come from other sources as well. The experiences of Folke Bernadotte and Dag Hammarskjöld as well as the better known Raoul Wallenberg were heroic but costly. War has many victims but so does peacemaking.

Nordic Influences and Nordic Sons

Herbert E. Gooch III, Ph.D.
California Lutheran University
Department of Political Science
Thousand Oaks, California

Much has been justly made of Nordic influences on the world stage by its native sons and daughters. It is only fitting to include an appreciation of their children in immigrant lands. Nowhere is this influence more in evidence than in America where the many distinctive Nordic values took root and grew to produce two of the most influential political figures of the late 20th century.

Christopher Warren, the 63rd U.S. Secretary of State during the Clinton years, was considered by the three presidents he served as one of the finest diplomats they ever met. At his death, he was described by President Obama as a "resolute pursuer of peace" for his work in the Middle East and the Balkans and by Hillary Clinton as a "diplomat's diplomat – talented, dedicated and exceptionally wise." As political adviser in domestic politics, he was highly respected in Democratic and national politics. As diplomat, he decisively helped shape America's role in the post-Cold War era.

Earl Warren came late in his life to being the Chief Justice of the Supreme Court, after a successful and famed role in California and national politics. As Chief Justice he led the Court between 1953 and 1969, and was successful in reshaping the landscape of American politics. The "Warren Court" is regarded as the most significant, and controversial, change agent of the last half of the 20th century. Its decisions eliminating segregation, providing for equal voting, and protecting the rights of the accused continue to affect and define the substance of political debate.

As sons of Nordic parents – Norway for Christopher and Norway and Sweden for Warren - it is no accident that particular values of equality, hard work, unpretentiousness, conflict avoidance, and preference for negotiation over conflict were so much in evidence in their approach to political practice. It is therefore worth reviewing their lives and accomplishments to remind us that Nordic influences have been carried by immigrants to new lands.

Warren Christopher (1925-2011): The Indispensable Man

Warren Christopher, 63rd United States Secretary of State during the Clinton years, was born of Norwegian immigrant stock in Scranton, North Dakota. The family's Norwegian roots and the practice of a strict Lutheranism formed a life-long penchant for self-effacement and hard work.

The collapse of the family fortune in the Depression led to a move to Southern California and a life-long political identification with the struggling underdog. He graduated from the University of Southern California before enlisting in the Navy in the closing days of WW II. Precocious and ambitious, he then attended Stanford Law School and was its first graduate to clerk for the U.S. Supreme Court (1949-1950). Justice William O. Douglas advised him to seek out a life of public service beyond the narrow legal profession, advice Christopher took to heart. His life would be a constant journeying between private practice and public service ranging over California, Washington, D.C. and the world for the remainder of his 85 years.

He practiced law with the prestigious Los Angeles-based law firm of O'Melveny & Myers (1950-1967), becoming a partner in 1958. Involvement in California state and local Democratic party affairs led to his serving as special counsel to Governor Pat Brown in Sacramento and appointment as U.S. Deputy Attorney General (1967-69) in Washington under President Lyndon Johnson. He rejoined O'Melveny & Myers, rose to senior partner, and became known as one of the most successful and prestigious litigators in California.

President Jimmy Carter recalled Christopher to Washington (1977-79) to employ his superb negotiating and management skills as U.S. Deputy Secretary of State. He was the point man negotiating Panama's sovereignty over the Panama Canal and in the return of the 52 American prisoners of the revolutionary regime of Iran. He was involved further in the General Agreement on Trade and Tariffs (GATT) and North American Free Trade Association (NAFTA) treaty negotiations, and was awarded the Medal of Freedom in 1981.

During the Reagan years, he returned to California and led the investigation and reform of law enforcement after the Rodney King domestic riots. With the election of Bill Clinton, he returned to Washington and the arena of world diplomacy as U.S. Secretary of State (1993-1997).

This was the era of peace between the two Gulf Wars against Saddam Hussein, peaceful times when Christopher guided American foreign policy and kept it remarkably free of armed conflict. A "New World Order" was settling into place where America was recognized not as unipolar hegemon over the globe, but as the indispensable nation amongst states, in dealing with the failed state of Somalia and genocide in Rwanda, and bringing all sides together to work out accords in Palestinian-Israeli relations and the Balkan Wars of the late 1990s.

For an administration and president lacking in foreign affairs experience, Christopher was indispensable. He favored a profile of moderation and international cooperation, elevating and enhancing the use of the "soft powers" of attraction and cooperation rather than relying on threat and force to compel obedience.

Among the accomplishments of his tenure were the Oslo Accords (the outlines of a Palestinian state and major step on what has remained a faltering and imperfect road towards peace), the Dayton Agreements (serving to end the Balkan Wars), normalization of U.S-Vietnamese relations, prodding China towards commitment to human rights, and efforts to sustain democracy in Haiti and end genocide in Rwanda.

Christopher was the diplomat's diplomat. Dressed impeccably, his reputation was that of a thoroughly prepared, capable and cautious man. As Secretary of State, he told *U.S. News & World Report* his "first priority" was to "attack problems before they reach the crisis level" and to keep the United States from expending lives and fortune in international disputes. "I'd much rather be known as somebody who was a preventer of crises than as a crisis manager," he said.

He could unravel the impossible into discrete threads of what might be possible, then weave these together to produce improbable agreements bringing all to understand that each might be better pulling together than pulling apart. He was always in the picture, but loath to take credit, satisfied with mutual results rather than individual fame. Characteristically, his stock answer to questions about his personal and public success was ever and simply, "I've been very lucky."

When others might despair, Warren Christopher pushed ahead, resolute in the conviction that, no matter the difficulty negotiation was better than confrontation, peace than violence, hope than despair. Writers and commentators characterized him as dour, attentive to - even obsessive about - detail, patient, steady and poised, but rarely, if ever, charismatic. Fashionably attired, faultlessly prepared, intellect and integrity were his calling cards. President Clinton once joked that Mr. Christopher was "the only man ever to eat presidential M&Ms with a knife and fork." No one was surprised when, on an official stopover in Ireland, he ordered Irish coffee, decaffeinated and without alcohol.

He referred to himself as a "steward," one whose true and underlying vocation is service to others. He did not need to stand out to serve. As Secretary of State, he sought to make America's role in world affairs indispensable rather than dominant or commandeering.

The recipient of honors too numerous to be cataloged here, Warren Christopher passed away in 2011, survived by his wife and four children from two marriages, and the admiration of those fortunate enough to have known him and the untold many whom he served. In President Jimmy Carter's memoires, he is described as simply "the best public servant I ever knew." He was an indispensable man.

Earl Warren (1891-1974): Equal Justice Under Law

Earl Warren was the son of a Norwegian father and a Swedish mother. The family was poor and his father, a railroad worker, often unemployed and absent. Born in rural California, young Earl applied himself in school and attended the University of California at Berkeley, and then studied law. He volunteered for service in WW I and after briefly working in private practice, in 1920 joined the County District Attorney's office. For the next 49 years he never left public service.

In 1925 he married Nina Palmquist Meyers, a widow, born in Sweden. With her he had five children and it is characteristic of the man that his grave marker in Arlington National Cemetery notes his service as an army lieutenant and his marriage to Nina, omitting that he happened also to have been Governor of the State of California three times, unsuccessful candidate for Vice-President of the United States, and Chief Justice of the U.S. Supreme Court. Talk about a Nordic penchant for understatement!

His hard work as a prosecuting district attorney led to advancement, and then election to the office of County District Attorney, where he earned a solid reputation as one of the "best district attorneys" in the state and nation. From that success, he built a solid base of political support in the Republican party which led him to run successfully for State Attorney General and then for an unprecedented three times (1942, 1946, 1950) as Governor of California. The last candidacy was undertaken under a system of cross-filing which allowed him to win both Democratic and Republican party preferences.

His fame and influence reached national proportions. He ran for Vice President with Tom Dewey in 1948 (unsuccessfully) and was a key broker of the choice of Dwight Eisenhower for President in 1952. That support led Eisenhower to propose him for Chief Justice of the Supreme Court in 1953. The conservative Ike would later claim that appointment was "the biggest damned-fool mistake I ever made." For as Chief Justice, Warren would journey further to a broader, more expansive and liberal interpretation of what the law should accomplish and how it should be applied than had been evident in his earlier career.

As Chief Justice, he worked tirelessly to build consensus, first made clear in the first significant, block-buster decision regarding racial discrimination (*Brown v. School Board of Topeka, Kansas*) of his tenure. The nine justices were deeply divided. Knowing the explosive national repercussions of the decision to outlaw school racial segregation, Warren took a year to slowly build consensus, even assigned himself the writing of the majority opinion and delivered a full nine votes. That decision reversed the 1896 *Plessy v. Ferguson* affirmation of legal segregation throughout the land. It stated simply that, "We conclude that, in the field of public education, the doctrine of 'separate but equal' has no place. Separate educational facilities are inherently unequal."

Over the next 15 years the "Warren court" would shake and mold the practice of law and structure of political life in fundamentally new directions. The decisions were wide-ranging and had the collective effect of reinforcing popular liberties and individual equality. Among these were rulings which:

- Outlawed school segregation.
- Enunciated the one-man, one-vote doctrine.
- Made most of the Bill of Rights binding on the states.
- Curbed wiretapping.
- Upheld the right to be secure against "unreasonable" searches and seizures.
- Buttressed the right to counsel.
- Underscored the right to a jury trial.
- Barred racial discrimination in voting, in marriage laws, in the use of public parks, airports and bus terminals and in housing sales and rentals.
- Extended the boundaries of free speech.
- Ruled out compulsory religious exercises in public schools.
- Restored freedom of foreign travel.
- Knocked out the application of both the Smith and the McCarran Acts-- both designed to curb "subversive" activities.
- Held that Federal prisoners could sue the Government for injuries sustained in jail.

- Said that wages could not be garnished without a hearing.
- Liberalized residency requirements for welfare recipients.
- Sustained the right to disseminate and receive birth control information.

It is instructive to note what Warren himself thought the most significant of the decisions and areas he helped guide the court to change. And it is interesting to reflect on their consistency with Nordic values. Looking back over his tenure, in retirement he ranked the three most important in the following order. For Warren the most significant decisions were in the area of structural reform of the voting system, the decisions implementing one man one vote. The critical decisions in this respect were those which (1) mandated the re-drawing of voting districts to be equal in size so that a vote in one district counts as much as in all similar districts (*Baker v. Carr*, 1962) and (2) eliminated the over-representation of rural districts in State legislatures by providing vote apportionment on the basis of people not place (*Reynolds v. Sims*, 1964). Regarding Reynolds he remarked, "The overriding objective must be substantial equality among the various districts, so that the vote of any citizen is approximately equal in weight to that of any other citizen in the state." Very simply, "Legislators represent people, not trees or acres. Legislators are elected by voters, not farms or cities or economic interests." His penchant for equality is nowhere better expressed than in his later musing,

> If everyone in this country has an opportunity to participate in his government on equal terms with everyone else, and can share in electing representatives who will be truly representative of the entire community and not some special interest, then most of the problems that we are confronted with would be solved through the political process rather than through the courts.

Interestingly, the Brown decision was in second place, despite unleashing a political maelstrom which has not subsided even today and causing a fundamental realignment of parties (ideologically and geographically the Republicans moving conservative and Southern).

In third place of importance, he pointed to a set of decisions ensuring equal rights before the law, the rights of the accused, and limiting police powers. For instance in the Escobedo, Miranda, and Gideon decisions, Warren argued that any and every individual accused of wrong-doing has inviolable rights which must be respected. Or as summed up in the Miranda (1964) decision, the accused, must be warned prior to any questioning that he has the right to remain silent, that anything he says can be used against him in a court of law, that he has the right to the presence of an attorney, and that, if he cannot afford an attorney one will be appointed for him prior to any questioning if he so desires.

Individuals have rights, over and against police and public authorities.

"I would like the Court to be remembered as the people's court," he remarked on his retirement, expressing his strong sense of indignation over wrongs done to obscure citizens in the Government's name. This was a quite different attitude from his earlier law-and-order views as a California prosecutor; but Mr. Warren had become more liberal with age and perspective. "On the Court I saw [things] in a different light," he once explained. He became more liberal, more tolerant of dissent, more inclined to look to equality of treatment before law, the rights of the common man and woman. But then he had always a streak of preference for fair and equal treatment. As Governor of California he supported Japanese internment in WW II, but he also proposed compulsory health care – a policy far too early for its time.

Warren's career consistently reflected certain qualities, a capacity for hard work, a disarming affability and self-effacing style, and an ideological progression from right to left. Justice Thurgood Marshall, then lead counsel for the Brown decision, noted the week after Warren's appointment as Chief Justice, he saw him walking in the hallway near his office when Warren noticed an awed worker snap to attention, went over to the man and greeted him, saying, "My name is Earl Warren – what's yours?"

He was no stranger to controversy. There were popular demonstrations against him, even cries for his impeachment. He said he was often proud to be attacked for what he so fervently believed should be the law, yet he responded with a low profile refusing to fan the fires of controversy. Until retirement, he was famous for neither accepting awards nor speaking out in the public arena, preferring to exercise influence behind the cloistered legal chambers. Thus he remarked one of the most difficult times for him was when in the aftermath of the Kennedy assassination President Johnson dragged him into the national spotlight to chair the commission investigating assassination. His reputation for probity was so great, and the occasion so dire, only his leadership had a chance to quell the national hysteria and (hopefully) end suspicion and controversy.

He retired from the court in 1969. Shortly before his death in 1974, he reflected,

Where there is injustice, we should correct it; where there is poverty, we should eliminate it; where there is corruption, we should stamp it out; where there is violence we should punish it; where there is neglect, we should provide care; where there is war, we should restore peace; and wherever corrections are achieved we should add them permanently to our storehouse of treasure.

On the Supreme Court building there is chiseled in marble, "Equal Justice Under Law," a phrase which neatly sums up Earl Warren's values, commitment and significance in American political life.

Appendix
Nordic Spirit Symposium Series History

February 2000	The Vikings: Westward Exploration, Expansion and Settlement
February 2001	The Vikings: Eastern Traders, Merchants, Empire Builders and Royal Guards
February 2002	Scandinavian Immigrants: Builders of Nations
February 2003	The Northern Front, Scandinavia in World War 2: Neutrality, Occupation and Resistance
February 2004	The Northern Front, Scandinavia in World War 2, Part 2
February 2005	The Swedish-Norwegian Union and the Emergence of Nordic Nationalism
February 2006	On the Cutting Edge: Leading Scientific, Technological, Environmental and Cultural Developments in the Nordic Countries
February 2007	Grieg, Genes and Global Reach
February 2008	Myths, Digs and Saga Kings: A New Look at the Viking Age
February 2009	Sagas and the Viking World
February 2010	The Nordic Explorers: From Polar Frontiers to the Silk Road
February 2011	The Nordic Explorers: Voyages, Expeditions and Discoveries
February 2012	After the Vikings – Before the Reformation: Scandinavia in Transition
February 2013	Scandinavian Peacemakers and Humanitarians
February 2014	Scandinavians in the Old West